THE
MOTIVATION
FORCE

THE
MOTIVATION FORCE

HOW TO MOTIVATE YOURSELF TO DO JUST ABOUT ANYTHING

WILLIAM U. PEÑA MBA

TABLE OF CONTENTS

PART 3. THE MOTIVATED LIFE

INTRODUCTION

WHY WRITE A BOOK on motivation? Because, like many people, you probably have things to do but can't seem to find the energy to do them. These aren't just small things either; they are important tasks like finishing work, exercising, or even spending time with family. You know that getting these things done will help you in the long run, but you just don't feel motivated to start.

What's interesting is that when we finally push ourselves to complete these tasks, we feel great. Not only do we feel accomplished, but we also see how much better our lives become because we finish them. Maybe you hit the gym a couple of times and feel stronger. Or maybe you finally completed that project at work, and it helped move your career forward. Yet, even with those good feelings and rewards, we still struggle to stay motivated consistently.

The big question this book aims to answer is simple: How can you find the motivation to do the things you know are important? And more than that, how can you keep doing them regularly, especially when you don't feel like it?

Many people turn to things outside of themselves for motivation, like accountability partners or rewards. However, the problem with external motivation is that it doesn't last. When the reward or pressure disappears, so does the drive.

WHY EXTERNAL MOTIVATION FAILS

External motivation works like a push from outside. You might join a gym because a friend invited you, or you get a new Fitbit to track your steps. These things help, but what happens when your friend stops going, or you forget to charge your Fitbit? Often, you end up right back where you started—without the drive to keep going.

Imagine this: You're trying to stick to a healthy diet, but one day, someone brings donuts to the office. All that motivation you had to eat healthy vanishes in a flash. This is what happens when we rely too much on external motivation. It can be easily disrupted by small changes in our environment. The motivation fades away because it was never really yours—it was borrowed from something outside of you.

THE POWER OF INTERNAL MOTIVATION

Internal motivation, on the other hand, is different. It comes from within and doesn't rely on outside forces. Think of something you love to do, like a hobby or activity that you've been committed to for years. Even without rewards or pressure, you keep doing it because it feels right.

This kind of motivation is powerful because it's deeply rooted in what matters to you. It can last for years and can help you overcome even the toughest challenges.

For example, let's say you've spent thousands of dollars and countless hours on a hobby, like photography or gardening. You don't need someone to remind you to work on it. You're driven by your own love and passion for it. That's what internal motivation feels like.

The goal of this book is to help you unlock that same kind of energy for all the things you need to do in life.

IMAGINE THE POSSIBILITIES

Take a moment to imagine what your life would look like if you could tap into this powerful force whenever you needed it. Picture yourself facing a difficult task, like finishing a big project at work, and being able to find the inner strength to not only start it but finish it quickly. What would that mean for you?

For me, finding this motivation allowed me to push my career to new heights. It helped me get in better shape. It gave me the confidence to take care of my responsibilities, whether at work or home. I no longer felt guilty for procrastinating, and I stopped letting people down. It gave me the confidence to make promises and know that I could keep them.

What would it mean for you? Maybe it would mean finally getting that promotion at work. Or maybe it would give you the energy to keep up with your kids, finish that home improvement project, or get in shape. Whatever it is, this internal motivation can help you become the person you've always wanted to be.

HOW DOES INTERNAL MOTIVATION WORK?

So, where does this internal motivation come from? At its core, it comes from a natural survival mechanism that we all have. Our bodies are built with a fight-or-flight response, which kicks in when we face danger. When something threatens us, our bodies flood with adrenaline, giving us the physical strength and motivation to either run away or fight.

Think about those incredible stories you hear in the news, like the person that ran into a burning building to save someone, or the person who lifted a car to rescue someone trapped underneath. These people didn't sit around thinking about whether they had the energy or motivation. They just acted, powered by this internal force that helped them accomplish what seemed impossible.

While most of us won't need to run into burning buildings or lift cars, we can still tap into this reservoir of motivation in everyday life. The key is learning how to trigger that same force when it's time to tackle important but less life-threatening tasks.

THE HIERARCHY OF MOTIVATION

Our internal motivation is tied to something called the "hierarchy of motivation." This is a system in our minds that helps us prioritize what's important. We are wired to focus on things that matter most to our survival and happiness. For example, avoiding pain, seeking pleasure, and protecting our identity are high on the list. Therefore, tasks that align with these priorities get more energy from us.

Let's say you have to do something boring, like your taxes. You know it's important, but it's not very exciting. So, what do you do instead? You might watch TV or take a nap—things that feel more rewarding in the short term. The problem is that doing your taxes isn't high on your internal motivation list. To get them done, you have to connect them to something higher up in the hierarchy.

For instance, if you remind yourself that not doing your taxes could lead to fines or an audit (pain), it becomes more urgent. Or, you might connect it to a larger goal, like achieving financial freedom (pleasure). This shifts the task higher on your list of priorities, making it easier to find the motivation to get it done.

YOU WERE BORN WITH THE TOOLS

The good news is that we already have everything we need to succeed. Since birth, we have within us the ability to harness this internal motivation to improve our lives. We just need to learn how to use it. This book is a guide that will teach you how to tap into this "Motivation Force" within you, and direct it toward the things that matter most.

Picture your life as a car, and your internal motivation is the engine. Right now, your car might be sitting in the driveway, waiting for a spark to get it moving. This book will give you the tools to start the engine, keep it running and help you get to your destination. You'll be able to drive toward your goals, whether that's improving your health, advancing your career, or building stronger relationships.

GET READY FOR CHANGE

By the time you finish this book, you'll know how to unlock your Motivation Force and apply it to any task, no matter how difficult or boring it may seem. You'll understand why motivation fades and how to reignite it when you need it most. You'll learn how to prioritize tasks and link them to your deeper values, making them more meaningful and easier to complete.

Most importantly, you'll discover that you have the power to create lasting change in your life. Whether you're chasing big dreams or just trying to get through your daily responsibilities, this book will help you find the motivation you need to get it done. So, buckle up and get ready for some radical growth and change.

Your Motivation Force is about to be unleashed!

PART 1

THE
MOTIVATION
FORCE

1

THE MOTIVATION FORCE

IT WAS A COLD winter day in a small village in northern Canada. Lydia Angyiou, a quiet 41-year-old mother of two, was outside near a youth center with her young boys. Everything seemed peaceful—until she saw a massive 9-foot polar bear staring at her children. In that moment, something inside Lydia switched on. She didn't think. She didn't run. She did what any loving mother would do—she charged straight at the bear.

Imagine that for a second. A tiny woman, only five feet tall and barely 90 pounds, going head-to-head with one of the most powerful animals on Earth. No weapon. No backup. Just pure love, fear, and unstoppable courage. Why would anyone do that? The answer is simple: her kids mattered more than her own safety.

A woman walking by saw Lydia kicking the bear and screamed in shock, "Polar bear!" A nearby child ran for help. A man grabbed a rifle and rushed to the scene. But by the time he got there, Lydia was already fighting the bear with her bare hands. It wasn't until he fired warning shots—and then finally had to put the bear down—that the danger ended. Lydia was covered in blood and in shock. But she was alive. And most importantly, her kids were safe.

When the police showed up, one of them said, "She saved her kids' lives." He added, "She's pretty quiet. I've known her for years, and I've never seen anything like this. But I guess when your back is against the wall, and your child's life is on the line, you find the strength."

This story teaches a powerful lesson. When something really matters to you, motivation becomes unstoppable. You don't need a pep talk. You don't need a to-do list. You just act. Because something inside of you—the deepest, strongest force takes over. It's not logic. It's not willpower. It's the force of love. Of purpose. Of urgency.

WHAT'S DRIVING YOU?

Have you ever had a moment when you were too tired or lazy to do something, but then something happened, and suddenly you got a burst of energy? Maybe you were sitting on the couch, too tired to clean the house, but then someone called and said they were coming over in ten minutes. Suddenly, you jumped up and cleaned the house faster than you thought possible. This kind of thing happens to all of us, and it shows that we already have a hidden energy inside us that can be unleashed when we need it.

This energy is what I call the *Motivation Force*. It's the force that pushes us to get things done, even when we don't feel like it. The question is, how can we tap into this Motivation Force whenever we need it, not just when there's an emergency? In this chapter, we'll talk about what the Motivation Force is, where it comes from, and how you can start using it to tackle your everyday tasks.

THE POWER OF MOTIVATION

Reading Lydia Angyiou's polar bear story reveals a common truth. When people are faced with life-or-death situations, their bodies react by giving them the energy and strength to do whatever it takes. That's the fight-or-flight response kicking in. When we're in danger, our bodies release adrenaline, and we suddenly find the strength to run faster or fight harder than we ever thought possible. This is one form of the Motivation Force—an instinct that helps us survive when we're threatened.

But here's the thing: You don't have to wait for a polar bear to attack you to tap into this energy. You can learn how to trigger this force whenever you need it. The same motivation that helped that mother protect her child can help you finish a big project, start a new workout routine, or finally clean out your garage.

THE SOURCE OF THE MOTIVATION FORCE

The Motivation Force comes from deep within us. It's a natural part of being human. We are programmed to prioritize things that are most important to us—our survival, our purpose, and our identity. When something is important enough, our bodies and minds will find the energy to get it done.

For example, think about how you feel when you're really hungry. Suddenly, all you can think about is finding food. You'll stop whatever you're doing to eat because your survival is at the top of your priority list. The same thing happens when we need to protect someone we love or avoid something painful. These situations are so important to us that we automatically find the energy to take action.

But not every task feels as urgent as survival or protecting someone we love. That's where the challenge comes in. How do we find the motivation to do things that aren't urgent but are still important, like finishing a work project or going to the gym? The key is to learn how to connect these tasks to something higher on your priority list.

THE HIERARCHY OF MOTIVATION

Our motivation works like a ladder, with the most important things at the top and less important things at the bottom. At the very top are things like survival, avoiding pain, and seeking pleasure. These are the things that naturally get the most energy and attention from us.

Below that, we have things like our sense of purpose and our iden-tity—how we see ourselves and what we believe in. These are also very important and can give us a lot of motivation when we connect them to the tasks we need to get done. Further down the ladder, we find things like habits and daily tasks that might not feel as urgent or important.

For example, let's say you need to do your taxes. It's not something you're excited about, so it's sitting low on your motivation ladder. But if you start thinking about the pain of getting audited or the pleasure of having your finances in order, suddenly, it moves up the ladder. Now, your brain starts to see it as more important, and you're more likely to find the energy to get it done.

TAPPING INTO THE MOTIVATION FORCE

Now that we understand where motivation comes from, the biggest question is: How do we tap into it?

The secret is to link the task you need to do with something higher on your motivation ladder. If you can connect a task to your survival, your sense of purpose, or your identity, you'll be able to unleash the power of the Motivation Force to help you get the job done.

For example, if you're struggling to start a big work project, think about why it's important. Maybe completing the project will help you advance in your career, which connects to your sense of purpose. Or maybe it will help you provide for your family, which ties into your survival instincts. By linking the task to something higher on your ladder, you'll naturally feel more motivated to start and finish it.

This process is like fixing a broken Christmas light. When one bulb is out, the whole string of lights goes dark. But once you fix the broken bulb, the entire string lights up again. In the same way, when you connect a task to something important, the energy to complete it lights up inside you.

EXAMPLES OF THE MOTIVATION FORCE IN ACTION

Let's go back to the example of the polar bear. That mother didn't have to sit and think about whether she had the energy to fight off the bear. Her Motivation Force kicked in automatically because protecting her child was at the top of her motivation ladder. She didn't need a plan or a pep talk; she just acted.

Now, think about a time in your own life when you felt extremely motivated to get something done. Maybe it was a moment when you had to protect someone, solve a big problem, or reach a major goal. In those moments, you probably felt a surge of energy, and nothing could stop you from achieving what you set out to do. That was your Motivation Force at work.

The challenge is to bring that same kind of motivation into your daily life, even when the stakes aren't as high. How can you get yourself to feel motivated to do things like clean the house, exercise, or finish work projects? By learning to tap into your Motivation Force, you can find the energy to do these things just as easily as if you were facing a life-or-death situation.

USING THE MOTIVATION FORCE FOR EVERYDAY TASKS

So, how do you use the Motivation Force for the things that aren't emergencies? The key is to link the task to something that's important to you. For example, if you need to clean the house but don't feel like it, think about how a clean home can give you a sense of peace and comfort. Or think about how it will make your family happy, which connects to your desire to take care of them.

The more you practice this, the easier it becomes. Soon, you'll be able to find the motivation for even the smallest tasks by connecting them to something higher on your ladder. It's all about changing the way you think about the task. Instead of seeing it as something boring or unimportant, you start to see it as a way to fulfill your bigger goals and values.

CONCLUSION
The Start of a New Journey

Tapping into the Motivation Force is like unlocking a hidden power within yourself. Once you learn how to access it, you'll find that you have the energy to do things you never thought possible. You'll no longer be held back by laziness or procrastination. Instead, you'll be able to tackle any task with confidence and purpose.

As we move forward in this book, we'll explore ways to activate your Motivation Force. You'll learn how to connect everyday tasks to your deeper values, how to overcome obstacles, and how to stay motivated even when things get tough. This is the start of a new journey for you—a journey toward becoming the best, most motivated version of yourself.

Let's get started!

2

WHAT IS MOTIVATION AND WHERE DOES IT COME FROM?

IT WAS A COLD January morning in 2007 in New York City. Wesley Autrey, a 50-year-old construction worker, was standing on a subway platform with his two young daughters when he noticed a man having a seizure. The man, Cameron Hollopeter, collapsed and fell onto the train tracks—just as the lights of an oncoming train appeared in the tunnel.

Without hesitation, Wesley jumped down onto the tracks. He knew he only had seconds. He pinned Cameron's body into the space between the rails and lay on top of him, holding him down so he wouldn't be struck by the train. Five train cars passed over them, missing them by mere inches. When the train stopped, the crowd went silent—until Wesley called out, "We're okay down here, but I've got two daughters up there. Let them know their father is okay."

Wesley's only thought was to save a life, even if it meant risking his own. He didn't plan it. He didn't wait.

He just acted.

WHAT DOES MOTIVATION COME FROM?

Motivation is the energy inside you that makes you want to do something. It's the feeling that pushes you to get up and take action, even when you don't feel like it.

But what exactly is motivation, and where does it come from?

In this chapter, we'll explore what motivation is. We'll break it down into small pieces so you can understand it and harness its power. By the end of this chapter, you'll see that motivation isn't some mysterious thing that comes and goes. Instead, it's something you can learn to control and increase whenever you need it.

A SIMPLE DEFINITION

There are many definitions of motivation, but let's keep it simple: Motivation is when your desire to do something is so strong that it helps you overcome any obstacles or challenges in your way. It's like having a strong enough reason that nothing can stop you from getting something done.

Imagine you need to clean your house, but you're feeling lazy. Then you find out that your girlfriend or boyfriend is coming over in an hour. Suddenly, you jump up and start cleaning, even though you didn't want to a minute ago. Why? Because now you have a big enough reason to get it done. That's motivation in action.

WHY THIS DEFINITION IS HELPFUL

This definition of motivation is helpful for a few reasons. First, it makes motivation something that's within your control. If motivation is just about having a strong enough desire, then you can find ways to increase that desire whenever you need to.

Second, it shows that motivation is also about overcoming obstacles. Sometimes, the obstacles are external, like time or physical effort. Other times, they're internal, like feeling tired or bored. If you can find a way to minimize the effect of those obstacles, it will give you the edge you need to push through those obstacles.

Lastly, this definition focuses on internal motivation, which doesn't depend on things outside of you. You don't have to wait for someone else to motivate you or for the perfect circumstances. You can learn to create your own motivation, no matter what's happening around you.

HOW TO INCREASE YOUR DESIRE

Now that we understand what motivation is, let's talk about how to increase it.

If motivation is about having a strong enough desire, then we need to find ways to grow that desire. Think about a time when you really wanted something—whether it was an experience, a goal, or even a person. What made you want it so much?

If you think back to when you were really motivated, you'll probably notice that what you were trying to achieve felt very important at the time. Which brings us to a critical principle of motivation:

 The more important something is, the more motivated we feel to get it done.

IMPORTANCE, DESIRE, AND MOTIVATION

Let's think about this with a simple formula: the more important something is to you, the more desire you'll have for it. And the more desire you have, the more motivation you'll create. It's like a chain reaction. If you can make something feel more important, you'll feel more motivated to get it done.

For example, let's say you're trying to finish a project at work. If you think about it as just another task, it might not feel very important.

But if you start thinking about how finishing this project could lead to a promotion or help your team succeed, it suddenly feels more important. As the importance grows, so does your desire to get it done, and soon, you'll feel more motivated to tackle it.

THE ROLE OF VALUE IN MOTIVATION

So, what makes something feel important to us? The answer is value. The more value something has, the more important it becomes, and the more motivated we feel to do it. If you think something is valuable, you're much more likely to spend time and energy on it.

For example, let's say you're trying to decide whether to go to the gym. If you don't see much value in working out, it's easy to skip it. But if you start thinking about the long-term health benefits, the energy boost, or how it helps you feel confident, it becomes more valuable. Once you see the value, you'll feel more motivated to go.

Therefore, we find this ultimate motivation principle at work:

 The more valuable something is to you, the more motivated you'll be to get it done.

When we feel like a task has high value, we're willing to work harder and push through obstacles to accomplish it.

CERTAINTY AND MOTIVATION

Another powerful factor that increases motivation is certainty. As humans, we crave certainty. We want to feel sure that our actions will lead to success. The more certain we feel about achieving our goal, the more motivated we become to work toward it.

Imagine you're learning a new skill, like playing the piano. If you've never played before, you might feel uncertain about whether you'll succeed. This uncertainty can lower your motivation because you're unsure if your hard work will pay off. But your certainty increases if you've had some success with other musical instruments or someone tells you they're sure you'll be good at it. As a result, you feel more motivated to keep practicing.

This gives us another core motivation principle:

 The more certain you are that something will work, the more motivated you'll be to do it.

Certainty removes doubt, and when you're sure you'll succeed, it's easier to find the energy to take action.

BUILDING YOUR MOTIVATION EQUATION

Now, we can combine all these pieces into a simple motivation equation. Motivation comes from two main sources: importance and certainty. When you increase the importance of a task and your certainty that you can achieve it, your motivation grows.

The equation looks like this:

 Importance × Certainty = Motivation.

The more important something is and the more certain you feel about succeeding, the higher your motivation will be. This formula works for just about anything you need to get done.

For example, if you need to study for an important exam, you can increase your motivation by reminding yourself how valuable passing the exam is. Maybe it will help you reach a career goal or improve your life in some way. You can also boost your motivation by building your certainty—reviewing past successes, studying with friends, or breaking the task into small, manageable steps.

Before you know it, you start the task—and as you make progress, your motivation increases. When you finally finish, you look back in surprise at how much easier the task was than you originally thought.

That's the Motivation Force in action.

CONCLUSION

Motivation Is Within Your Reach

Motivation isn't something mysterious that you have to wait for. It's a combination of desire, importance, and certainty. By increasing the value of the tasks in front of you and building your certainty that you can succeed, you'll find the motivation you need to get things done.

You now have a simple formula for boosting your motivation whenever you need it:

Importance × Certainty = Motivation.

Start using this formula today to tackle your to-do list, work on your goals, and make progress in every area of your life. You'll be amazed at how much more motivated you feel when you understand where motivation comes from and how to create it within yourself.

Now let's discuss how to overcome the biggest obstacles to motivation.

3

THE MAIN OBSTACLE TO MOTIVATION

IN JULY 2018, Angela Hernandez was driving down California's Highway 1 when she swerved to avoid a small animal. Her Jeep slid off the edge and tumbled 250 feet down a cliff into the ocean. No one saw her fall. Her car was smashed, and she was badly hurt. But she was alive.

Angela had a brain injury, broken ribs, and her shoes were gone. For seven days, she survived by drinking water from her car's radiator and eating wild plants. Her phone didn't work. Her body was in pain. She had no way to call for help. But every day, she crawled up the rocky cliffs, little by little, hoping someone would see her.

On the seventh day, two hikers finally spotted her. "We could barely believe she was alive," they said. But Angela was alive—because she never gave up.

What made Angela keep going, against all odds, when everything inside her was telling her to stop?

The answer is that her desire to live overpowered her desire for relief.

THE BIGGEST OBSTACLE TO MOTIVATION

Even when we understand what motivation is and where it comes from, there's still one big challenge we must overcome: sometimes, we know we should do something, but we just can't get ourselves to do it. This is the biggest obstacle to motivation. It's like an invisible wall that stands between us and the things we need to get done. In this chapter, we're going to look at what that wall is made of and how we can finally break through it.

This obstacle doesn't come from outside. It's inside us. Sometimes, it feels like there are two parts of us pulling in different directions. One part wants to get things done, and the other part just wants to relax or do something more fun. This creates an inner battle that can stop us from making progress.

Understanding this battle is the first step to overcoming it.

THE INTERNAL TUG OF WAR

You've probably felt this tug-of-war before. Let's say you need to do your homework or pay your bills, but at the same time, you really want to watch TV or take a nap. Both sides are pulling at you, and you feel stuck in the middle. This internal battle can make it hard to find the energy or motivation to do what you know you need to do.

This tug-of-war happens because we have different desires inside of us. One part of you knows that doing your homework or paying your bills is important, while the other part just wants to avoid the boredom and stress that come with it. The result? You feel stuck, and nothing gets done.

THE MOTIVATION SEESAW

The best metaphor to describe this internal battle is like having two kids on a seesaw. The heavier kid (the stronger desire) always wins. If your desire to watch TV is stronger than your desire to do your homework or pay your bills, the seesaw will tip in favor of TV. But if you can make your desire to do your homework or pay bills stronger, the seesaw will tip the other way, and you'll find the motivation to get it done.

The seesaw is a simple but powerful way to understand motivation. On one side, you have the task you need to do. On the other side, you have all the things that are distracting you or pulling you away from the task. Whichever side is heavier wins.

For example, if you're trying to work on a project but your phone keeps buzzing with notifications, the distractions might feel heavier. Your desire to check your phone is stronger than your desire to focus on the project, so the seesaw tips in favor of the distraction. But if you remind yourself of why the project is important, you can add weight to that side of the seesaw and make it tip in your favor.

The goal isn't to make distractions go away completely. That's impossible. The goal is to make the task feel more important and exciting than the distractions. When you do that, you tip the seesaw in your favor, and suddenly, you feel motivated to get the task done.

WHY WE AVOID HARD TASKS

One reason the seesaw tips in favor of distractions is that we naturally avoid things that are hard, boring, or uncomfortable. It's part of our survival instinct. Our brains are wired to avoid pain and seek pleasure. This instinct kept our ancestors alive by helping them avoid danger and find food.

But in today's world, this instinct can make it hard to stay motivated. For example, balancing your budget doesn't seem connected to survival, so your brain labels it as a low priority. On the other hand, watching TV or scrolling through your phone gives you quick hits of pleasure, so your brain prioritizes those activities.

HOW TO TIP THE SEESAW IN YOUR FAVOR

So, how do you tip the seesaw in your favor? The answer lies in changing the way you think about the task. If you can connect the task to something that feels more important or rewarding, you'll add weight to that side of the seesaw. This will help you overcome the distractions and find the motivation to get it done.

For example, let's say you need to go to the gym, but you don't feel like it. If you think of the gym as just hard work, your brain will want to avoid it. But if you remind yourself that going to the gym will help you feel stronger, improve your health, help you feel more attractive, and give you more energy, the gym suddenly feels more meaningful. Now, the seesaw starts to tip in favor of going to the gym.

Another way to tip the seesaw in your favor, is to make the distractions feel less important. For example, if watching TV is distracting you from doing a task, you can remind yourself that watching TV is stealing your valuable and limited time, and it isn't helping you reach your goals. It might be fun at the moment, but it's not getting you any closer to the life you want. By making the distractions feel less important, you take weight off that side of the seesaw.

THE IMPORTANCE OF DESIRE

Ultimately, desire is at the heart of motivation. Therefore, the seesaw tips in favor of the task when your desire to accomplish it is stronger than your desire to avoid it. This is why it's so important to find ways to increase your desire for the things you need to do.

For example, if you need to write a report for work, you might not feel much desire to do it at first. But if you remind yourself that finishing the report will help you get closer to a promotion, getting you a raise, or improving your skills, your desire to do it increases. You start to see the task as more valuable, and that makes it easier to find the motivation to get started.

The good news is that desire isn't something you have to wait for. You can create it by focusing on the benefits of completing the task and connecting it to your bigger goals. In the following chapters we will discuss how to practice increasing your desire, so the easier it becomes to tip the seesaw in your favor.

OVERCOMING INTERNAL RESISTANCE

As mentioned previously, internal resistance is the feeling that comes up when part of you wants to do something, but another part of you doesn't. This resistance can make even the simplest tasks feel overwhelming.

For example, you need to clean the house, but you just don't feel like it. Part of you knows it's important, but another part of you would rather relax. This internal conflict can feel like you're stuck in place.

One way to lower resistance is to break the task into smaller, more manageable steps. Instead of cleaning the whole house, focus on cleaning one room or even just one corner of a room. When the task feels smaller, it's easier to get started—and the seesaw will be easier to tip in your favor. And once you get started, it's easier to keep going.

MAKING THE HARD TASKS EASIER

Another way to overcome internal resistance is to make the hard tasks feel easier. One way you can do this is by focusing on the rewards from completing the task. For example, if you're struggling to finish a project at work, think about how good it will feel to complete it, how relieved you will feel when it's over, and how it will help you move forward in your career.

You can also make tasks easier by setting a timer and committing to just a few minutes of work. Often, the hardest part is getting started. Once you've begun, it's much easier to keep going. This is because starting creates momentum, and that momentum can carry you through the rest of the task.

Finally, you can make tasks feel easier by celebrating small wins along the way. Instead of waiting until the entire task is done to feel good, give yourself a reward like a pat on the back, a simple check mark on your to-do list, or a chocolate treat for each step you complete. These small celebrations help build positive feelings around the task, making it easier to stay motivated.

CONCLUSION

Winning the Battle Inside

The biggest obstacle to motivation isn't the tasks themselves—it's the internal tug of war that happens when part of you wants to do something, and another part wants to avoid it. By understanding how the Motivation Seesaw works, you can start tipping it in your favor. You do this by increasing your desire for the task and lowering the importance of distractions.

Remember, motivation is all about desire. The more you focus on the benefits of getting the task done, the more motivated you'll feel. And as you practice these strategies, you'll find that it becomes easier to overcome resistance and get things done, even when the task feels hard or boring. This is how you win the battle inside and take control of your motivation.

Now let's learn how to tap into the two greatest motivation drivers.

4

THE FIRST TWO GREAT MOTIVATION DRIVERS: PLEASURE AND PAIN

AT OVER 400 POUNDS, David Smith was slowly dying. He felt like a prisoner in his own body. Breathing was hard. Stairs were impossible. Mirrors were the enemy. Years of emotional eating had buried him in pain—physically, mentally, and spiritually.

He had given up on hope. Until one day, a painful thought hit him like lightning:

"If I keep going like this, I'll never walk my daughter down the aisle."

That moment changed everything.

He didn't start with a gym membership or a diet plan. He started with a 30-second walk to the mailbox. He started with the pain of missing out—and the dream of being there for the most important day of her life.

Day by day, he added one more healthy habit. He lost 50 pounds, then 100... then 200.

When asked how he stayed motivated, he said:

"I stopped focusing on how much it hurt. I focused on who I was doing it for."

The pain of regret and the pleasure of a future memory—walking his daughter down the aisle—became his fuel. It wasn't about discipline. It was about desire.

This chapter is about that very power. The push of pain. The pull of pleasure. And how to turn both into a fire that never burns out.

THE POWER OF PAIN AND PLEASURE

Why do we do what we do?

A big part of motivation comes from two simple forces: pleasure and pain. These two drivers control much of our behavior without us even realizing it. We naturally move toward things that bring us pleasure and try to avoid things that bring us pain. This push and pull between pleasure and pain is powerful, and when we understand how it works, we can use it to motivate ourselves to get things done.

Think about it. When something seems fun, exciting, or enjoyable, it's easy to do. You don't need to force yourself to play your favorite game or eat your favorite food. You're naturally drawn to those things because they bring you pleasure. On the other hand, when something feels hard, boring, or painful, you naturally want to avoid it.

But what if we could use this same pleasure-pain system to motivate us to do the tasks we usually avoid?

SEEKING PLEASURE, AVOIDING PAIN

Pleasure and pain are two sides of the same coin. We are always trying to get more of the things that make us feel good and less of the things that make us feel bad. This is true whether we're talking about physical comfort, like eating good food or resting, or emotional comfort, like feeling loved or successful.

Imagine you have a big project due at work. You might feel stressed about it, which causes pain, so you put it off by scrolling on social media or doing something else that brings you pleasure. The problem is that the project is still hanging over your head, and the longer you avoid it, the more stressed you feel. The pain gets worse because you're avoiding the task. The key is to reverse this process—find a way to make the task more pleasurable and reduce the pain of avoiding it.

For example, you can remind yourself of how good it will feel to finish the project and be free from stress. You can picture the relief and satisfaction you'll experience once it's done. By focusing on the pleasure of completing the task, you can tip the Motivation Seesaw in your favor and start working on it. At the same time, think about the pain you're causing yourself by putting it off. The more you associate procrastination with pain, the less likely you'll be to avoid the task.

USING PLEASURE TO GET THINGS DONE

One of the easiest ways to motivate yourself is to add pleasure to the task. If you can find a way to make a boring or difficult task more enjoyable, you'll be more likely to do it. For example, if you need to exercise but don't feel like it, you can add something fun to the activity, like listening to your favorite music or watching a TV show while you work out. Suddenly, the task becomes more enjoyable because you've linked it with something that brings you pleasure.

Another way to use pleasure is to give yourself a reward when you finish a task. This could be something small, like treating yourself to a favorite snack or taking a break to do something fun. When you know there's a reward waiting for you at the end, the task feels less painful and more motivating. Your brain starts to connect the task with the pleasure of the reward, making it easier to get started.

Imagine a child who doesn't want to clean their room. But once their parent joins them and make it fun (by converting their clothes and hamper into a basketball court), suddenly, it doesn't seem so bad. The pleasure of the reward outweighs the pain of the chore. Adults work the same way. If you can link a task with a reward, you'll find it easier to motivate yourself to do it.

TURNING PAIN INTO A MOTIVATOR

Pain can be a powerful motivator, too, but not in the way we usually think. Most of the time, we try to avoid pain. But if we focus on the pain of not doing something, it can actually push us to take action. This is especially true when we're dealing with tasks that have long-term consequences. The discomfort from avoiding important responsibilities can build up and become even more painful than the task itself. If we can learn to focus on this pain, we can use it to motivate ourselves.

For example, think about your finances. You might put off organizing your budget because it feels boring or overwhelming. But if you focus on the pain of what could happen if you don't manage your money—like getting into debt or struggling to pay bills—that pain becomes a strong motivator. You start to see that the discomfort of doing the task now is much smaller than the pain of ignoring it. This shift in thinking can push you to take action.

Similarly, when you procrastinate on a work project, the thought of missing a deadline, disappointing your boss, or getting fired creates a painful consequence. If you focus on that, you can use the discomfort to drive yourself to start the task. The fear of these negative outcomes becomes a source of energy, pushing you forward.

BALANCING PLEASURE AND PAIN

The key to using pleasure and pain effectively is finding the right balance. If you focus only on the pain of avoiding a task, you might feel anxious or stressed, which can make it harder to start. On the other hand, if you focus only on the pleasure of finishing, you might not feel enough urgency to get moving. The trick is to use both forces together.

Start by thinking about the rewards of completing the task. Visualize the pleasure and satisfaction you'll feel when it's done. Then, shift your focus to the pain of avoiding the task. Think about the stress, frustration, or consequences that will come from putting it off. By holding both the pleasure and pain in your mind at the same time, you create a powerful push-and-pull effect that drives you to act.

For example, let's say you need to prepare a presentation, but you've been procrastinating. First, picture the relief and pride you'll feel when it's finally done. Then, think about the pressure of rushing at the last minute or the embarrassment of giving a poorly prepared presentation. This combination of pleasure and pain helps tip the Motivation Seesaw in your favor, making it easier to start.

PRACTICAL WAYS TO USE PLEASURE AND PAIN

Now that you understand how pleasure and pain work together to motivate you, here are some practical ways to use them in your daily life:

1. **Create a reward system:** Before you start a task, decide on a small reward for when you finish. This could be something like watching an episode of your favorite show, having a treat, or taking a relaxing break. Knowing there's a reward waiting for you adds pleasure to the task and makes it feel less daunting.

2. **Visualize the benefits:** Spend a few moments visualizing the positive outcomes of completing your task. Picture how good it will feel to check it off your list, and think about how it will help you move closer to your goals. This helps you focus on the pleasure of getting it done.

3. **Make the task more enjoyable:** If a task feels boring, find ways to add pleasure to it. Listen to music, work in a comfortable space, or break it into smaller parts so it feels easier. By making the task more fun, you reduce the resistance to starting it.

4. **Focus on the consequences of not doing it:** If you find yourself avoiding a task, take a moment to think about the pain of putting it off. What will happen if you don't complete it? How will you feel tomorrow if you keep procrastinating? This discomfort can help push you into action.

5. **Set a deadline:** Deadlines create a sense of urgency, which can trigger both pleasure and pain. The pleasure comes from knowing you're on track to finish, and the pain comes from the pressure of not meeting the deadline. Use this combination to stay focused and motivated.

CONCLUSION

Using Pleasure and Pain to Stay Motivated

Pleasure and pain are natural forces that guide much of our behavior. By understanding how these drivers work, you can use them to motivate yourself to get things done. The key is to find the right balance—focus on the pleasure of completing a task but don't ignore the pain of avoiding it. When you use both forces together, you create a powerful motivator that can push you to take action, even when you don't feel like it.

Motivation doesn't always have to be about forcing yourself to do something unpleasant. You can make tasks more enjoyable by adding fun elements, rewarding yourself, and focusing on the positive outcomes. At the same time, use the discomfort of avoiding tasks to give you the push you need to get started. When you master the balance between pleasure and pain, you'll find that motivation comes more easily, and getting things done feels less like a struggle and more like a natural part of your day.

Now let's discuss two other powerful drivers that you can add to your motivation tool belt.

5

THE NEXT TWO GREAT MOTIVATION DRIVERS: IMPORTANCE AND CERTAINTY

AT 2 A.M., Carmen Tarleton was sleeping peacefully when her world turned into a nightmare.

Her abusive ex-husband broke into her home, held her down, and poured industrial-strength lye all over her face and body. The pain was immediate and unimaginable. Her skin melted. Her eyesight was gone. She was burned over 80% of her body. Doctors gave her little chance to survive.

She couldn't walk. She couldn't see. She had no lips, no ears, no eyelids. She looked like a ghost of her former self.

But Carmen made a decision: "I'm going to live. And I'm going to matter."

That one decision changed everything.

The pain was unspeakable. The odds were low. But the importance of being a mother to her daughters... of reclaiming her voice... of proving that her story wasn't over — that was her fuel.

She said, "I may never look the same again, but I'm still me. And I still have something to give."

She went through over 60 surgeries, months of rehab, and years of emotional healing.

She didn't start with big leaps. She started with tiny wins. Sitting up. Standing. Taking a single step. Every small success added just a little more confidence. That's how she rebuilt her certainty—one brick at a time.

Years later, Carmen became one of the first people in the world to receive a full face transplant. She now travels the country, sharing her story of hope, healing, and the power of never giving up.

This chapter is about how those two forces, importance and certainty, can provide us with the addiitonal motivation we need to succeed.

IMPORTANCE X CERTAINTY = MOTIVATION

We've learned that pleasure and pain are powerful motivators, but they're only part of the picture. Two other drivers have a huge impact on our motivation: *importance* and *certainty*. As we mentioned at the beginning of this book, these drivers help us decide which tasks matter most and how likely we are to succeed at them. The more important something is to us and the more certain we are that we can do it, the more motivated we'll be to take action.

Think about a time when you had a big goal that felt important to you. Maybe it was getting a promotion, finishing a degree, or planning a special event for your family. Because this goal mattered to you, you were willing to put in the time and effort to make it happen. Importance motivated you to push through the challenges and keep going until you succeeded. Certainty played a role, too—if you believed you could achieve your goal, you were more likely to stick with it.

WHY IMPORTANCE DRIVES MOTIVATION

Importance is all about how much something matters to you. The more important a task feels, the more likely you are to put in the effort to get it done. If you think of a task as unimportant or low priority, you'll probably keep pushing it off, even if you know it needs to be done. On the other hand, if you can link the task to something you care deeply about, it will feel more urgent, and you'll be more motivated to complete it.

Let's say you have to write a report for work, but you're not feeling motivated. If you think of it as just another task on your to-do list, it might not feel very important. But what if you start thinking about how finishing this report will help you feel the pride of a job well done or move you closer to a promotion? The report feels more important because it's connected to your larger goals. As a result, you feel more motivated to get started.

Importance is like adding a 100lb weight to the Motivation Seesaw. Increasing the importance of a task tips the seesaw in your favor, making it easier to take action. The key is to find a way to connect the task at hand to something that matters to you personally.

FINDING IMPORTANCE IN EVERYDAY TASKS

Even tasks that seem boring or unimportant can be linked to something meaningful. The trick is to ask yourself, a simple question:

 "Why does this matter?"

For example, if you need to clean the house but don't feel like it, ask yourself: "Why does this matter?" Then, consider how a clean home can bring you peace, reduce stress, and make you feel more organized. Or think about how your family will appreciate having a tidy space. Suddenly, the task feels more important because it's tied to something meaningful you care about.

Another way to increase the importance of a task is to think about the long-term benefits, by asking:

 "What will completing this task do for me in the future?"

If you're working on a big project, remind yourself of how finishing it will help you reach your goals. If you're exercising, think about the health benefits you'll enjoy down the road. Focusing on the future rewards makes the task feel more important in the present.

Importance is among the most powerful motivation drivers because it taps into our values and goals. When something is important to us, and we identify with it—we're willing to work harder and push through obstacles to get it done.

THE ROLE OF CERTAINTY IN MOTIVATION

Certainty is the second driver that plays a big role in motivation. Certainty is all about how confident you feel that you can succeed at a task. If you're sure you can do something, you'll be more motivated to start and finish it. But if you're not sure whether you'll succeed, it's easy to feel stuck and avoid the task altogether.

Imagine you're learning to play the guitar. If you've never played before, you might feel uncertain about whether you'll be any good. That uncertainty can make it harder to practice because you're not sure if it's worth the effort. But if you've had some small successes—maybe you learned a few chords or played a simple song—you start to feel more certain that you can improve. As your certainty grows, so does your motivation to keep practicing.

Certainty gives us the confidence to take action. When we feel sure that we can succeed, we're more likely to start the task, stick with it, and finish it. The challenge is to build certainty, especially when we're facing something new or difficult.

BUILDING CERTAINTY ONE STEP AT A TIME

One of the best ways to increase certainty is to break the task into smaller, more manageable steps. If a task feels too big or overwhelming, it's easy to doubt yourself. But when you focus on one small step at a time, it feels more doable. Each small success builds your confidence, making it easier to keep going.

For example, if you're writing a long paper, don't think about the entire project at once. Instead, focus on writing one paragraph or doing a little bit of research. Once you complete that small step, you'll feel more certain that you can finish the rest. This step-by-step approach makes big tasks feel less intimidating and helps you build the certainty you need to stay motivated.

Another way to build certainty is by looking at past successes. Think about a time when you faced a challenge and overcame it. Reminding yourself of what you've already accomplished can boost your confidence and help you believe that you can succeed again. Even if the task in front of you is new, you can draw on your past experiences to feel more certain that you have what it takes to get it done.

INCREASING CERTAINTY IN EVERYDAY TASKS

You can apply the power of certainty to everyday tasks as well. Often, daily tasks feel the hardest to start, not because they're difficult, but because we doubt our ability to make them feel worth the effort. This is where increasing your certainty comes in handy. By breaking tasks down to a micro level (think 2-5 minute tasks), and focusing on small wins, you'll boost your confidence and find it easier to stay motivated, even with simple tasks like doing laundry or organizing your workspace.

For example, if you need to clean out your garage, start by organizing just one small area that will take 5 minutes. Once that's done, you'll see progress and feel more certain that you can handle the rest. Or, if you need to start exercising but feel uncertain about your fitness level, begin with a short 5 minute workout that's easy to complete. As you build on these small wins, your certainty grows, and the task becomes less intimidating.

It's important to remember that certainty doesn't mean you have to be perfect. It just means you need to believe in your ability to make progress, no matter how small. Each step forward builds your confidence, and that confidence fuels your motivation to keep going.

PRACTICAL TIPS TO BUILD IMPORTANCE AND CERTAINTY

Here are some practical ways to apply importance and certainty to your daily life:

1. **Find the meaning in your tasks:** Before starting a task, ask yourself: "Why does this matter?" Or, "How will this help me reach my goals or benefit my life in the future?" By connecting the task to something important, you'll feel more motivated to do it.

2. **Break tasks into smaller steps:** When a task feels too big, break it down into manageable pieces. Focus on completing one step at a time, and celebrate each small success. This builds your certainty and keeps your motivation strong.

3. **Remind yourself of past successes:** Think about the challenges you've faced before and how you overcame them. Use these memories to boost your confidence and remind yourself that you can handle the task ahead.

4. **Visualize your success:** Spend a few moments picturing yourself completing the task and feeling proud of your achievement. This helps build certainty and gives you the confidence to get started.

CONCLUSION

The Power of Importance and Certainty

Importance and certainty are two of the most powerful drivers of motivation. When something feels important, we're willing to work harder and push through obstacles to get it done. And when we feel certain that we can succeed, we're more likely to start, stick with, and finish the task.

By applying these drivers to your daily life, you can create a strong foundation for motivation. Whether you're tackling big goals or managing everyday tasks, the combination of importance and certainty will help you stay motivated and focused. The more you practice building these drivers, the easier it will be to get things done and move closer to your goals.

Remember, motivation is something you can create. It's not about waiting for the right moment or the perfect feeling. By increasing the importance of a task and building your confidence through small steps and past successes, you can tap into your Motivation Force and take action whenever you need to.

6

THE POWER OF LINKING

THE YEAR WAS 1968. The world's eyes were on Mexico City, where the Olympic Games were in full swing. The high-altitude marathon was underway, and athletes from every corner of the globe pushed themselves to their physical limits.

Among them was John Stephen Akhwari, a proud and hopeful long-distance runner from Tanzania. He had trained for years to represent his nation—his people—on the world stage. For him, this wasn't just a race. It was a mission.

But just a few miles into the 26.2-mile course, disaster struck.

Akwari was jostled in a group of runners, lost his footing, and crashed hard onto the pavement. His knee was dislocated, his shoulder scraped raw, and his leg began to bleed heavily. As he lay crumpled on the road, medical personnel rushed to him.

He got up, limping, grimacing, his face etched with pain, and began to hobble off the field.

Hours passed. The sun dipped lower.

The medalists had already been crowned. The stadium had mostly emptied. The crowd thinned, the lights dimmed, the noise faded.

And then, something miraculous happened.

A hush swept over the half-empty stadium as the announcer's voice crackled over the loudspeaker:

"Ladies and gentlemen... one more runner is entering the stadium."

All heads turned. And there he was—John Stephen Akhwari, dragging his injured leg, his body wrapped in makeshift bandages, sweat and blood streaking his face. Each step looked like agony. But he kept moving.

The crowd rose to their feet and roared with applause—not because he was first, but because he had the courage to finish.

When reporters asked why he didn't just quit like so many others, his words echoed through history:

"My country did not send me 5,000 miles to start the race.They sent me 5,000 miles to finish the race."

At some point, he associated his pain with a purpose. He linked his suffering to something bigger. That link, between the task and its deeper meaning is what carried him across the finish line.

Let's explore how you can tap into this same powerful force to stay motivated—even when everything in you wants to give up.

LINKING: THE SECRET TO UNLIMITED MOTIVATION

Motivation is something we all want more of, especially when we have important things to do. We've already learned about the major drivers of motivation: pleasure, pain, importance, and certainty. But there's a special tool we can use to make those drivers work even better. That tool is called *linking*.

Linking is like a secret key that helps us connect tasks we don't want to do with things that naturally motivate us. Once we understand how to use linking, we can tap into our internal motivation force at any time.

Linking works by connecting a task we need to do with something that already feels important, certain, or pleasurable to us. When we create this connection, it makes the task feel more meaningful, and we become more motivated to do it. Think of linking like tying two things together: one is the task, and the other is something we care about or enjoy. The stronger the link, the more energy we can access to get the task done.

THE POWER OF ASSOCIATION

The idea of linking comes from a psychological concept called *association*. Association happens when two things become connected in our minds because we experience them together. A famous example of this is Pavlov's dogs. In the early 1900s, a scientist named Ivan Pavlov discovered that when he rang a bell every time he fed his dogs, the dogs eventually began to associate the sound of the bell with food. Soon, just hearing the bell made the dogs salivate, even if there was no food.

We experience this kind of association all the time. For example, if you hear a song that was popular when you were in high school, it might bring back memories of your teenage years. Or if you smell a certain perfume, it might remind you of a person you care about. These connections happen because our brains are wired to link things together when we experience them at the same time.

The good news is that we can use this power of association to help us get things done. By linking a task we need to do with something that is highly motivating to us, we can transfer that energy and motivation to the task. This makes the task feel less like a burden and more like something we want to do.

HOW LINKING WORKS

Let's look at how linking can work in real life. Suppose you have a task that you've been avoiding, like organizing your closet. You know it needs to be done, but it feels boring and overwhelming. Instead of forcing yourself to do it, you can use linking to make the task feel more motivating.

Start by thinking about something that naturally motivates you. Maybe you love listening to music or podcasts. Now, link that enjoyable activity to the task by deciding that you'll listen to your favorite playlist while you organize the closet. By doing this, you're linking the task to something that feels pleasurable. Suddenly, the task doesn't seem so bad because you've added something enjoyable to it.

Another way linking works is by connecting a task to something valuable to you. Let's say you're trying to exercise regularly, but you find it hard to stay motivated. Instead of thinking about exercise as just something you "have to do," link it to your larger goal of staying healthy and having more energy for your family. By connecting the task to something valuable to you, you make it feel more important, and your motivation to exercise will increase.

USING QUESTIONS TO CREATE LINKS

One of the most powerful ways to create links between tasks and motivation is by asking the right questions. When we ask ourselves questions, our brains naturally start searching for answers and connections. This process helps us find ways to link the task we need to do with things that already motivate us.

For example, let's say you need to finish a work project, but you're having trouble getting started. You can ask yourself, "How will finishing this project help me in the future?" or "What will completing this task do for my career?" By asking these questions, you help your brain make connections between the task and the rewards that come from doing it. These connections make the task feel more important, and your motivation to complete it will increase.

Another example could be if you need to clean your house. You might not feel like it, but you can ask yourself, "How will I feel when my home is clean and organized?" or "How will cleaning my house benefit my family?" By answering these questions, you link the task to the pleasure of a clean space and the importance of taking care of your family. This gives you the push you need to get started.

MAKING THE TASK MEANINGFUL

One of the most powerful ways to use linking is to make tasks feel more meaningful. When we see a task as connected to something important, we naturally feel more motivated to do it. For example, if you have to complete a boring work assignment, you can link it to your bigger goals. Ask yourself, "How will doing this task help me grow in my skillset and make me more valuable?" or "How does this task support the overall success of my team?" By making the task part of a larger goal, you give it more meaning.

Another way to make a task meaningful is to link it to your values. Suppose you're struggling to keep up with an exercise routine. If one of your values is living a healthy, balanced life, you can link your workouts to that value. Ask yourself, "How does exercising reflect the kind of person I want to be?" or "How does this task help me live according to my values?" When a task aligns with your personal values, it feels more important, and it becomes easier to find the motivation to do it.

TAPPING INTO CERTAINTY THROUGH LINKING

We mentioned earlier how certainty is another important driver of motivation. When we feel certain that we can accomplish something, we're more likely to take action. Linking can help us tap into that sense of certainty by reminding us of past successes or breaking down tasks into smaller steps.

For example, let's say you're feeling uncertain about a big project at work. You can use linking to boost your confidence by asking yourself, "When have I successfully completed a similar project before?" By linking the task to past successes you increase your certainty that you can get it done.

When tasks feel overwhelming, linking helps you connect to smaller, more achievable goals. One way is by asking, "What steps can I take to make this task feel more manageable?" This makes the task feel less daunting and gives you the certainty you need to move forward. Each small success you experience builds your confidence, making it easier to keep going.

THE POWER OF LINKING IN ACTION

Let's take a look at how linking can work in a common work situation. Imagine you've been putting off a difficult conversation with a coworker. You know the conversation is important, but you're nervous about it. To motivate yourself, you can use linking to connect the task with the benefits that will come from having the conversation.

Ask yourself, "How will this conversation improve our working relationship?" or "What will be the positive outcome of addressing this issue?" By focusing on the positive results, you link the task to something valuable. This makes the task feel more important and gives you the motivation to face the challenge.

You can also use linking to make the conversation feel less intimidating. Break the task down into smaller steps, like planning what you'll say or setting up a time to talk. As you complete each small step, you build certainty that you can handle the conversation, and your confidence grows.

LINKING AND THE MOTIVATION SEESAW

Linking is one of the most powerful ways to tip the Motivation Seesaw in your favor. When you connect a task to pleasure, importance, or certainty, you add just enough weight to the side of action to get the job started. And as we've all experienced, starting is sometimes all it takes to create enough momentum to get the job done.

For example, if you've been putting off a task like writing a report, you can use linking to make the task feel more rewarding. Ask yourself, "What pleasure will I get from finishing this report?" or "How will completing this task help me reach my ultimate goal?" These questions help you find links that make the task feel more valuable and increase your desire to get started and get it done.

The power of linking is like flipping a switch in your brain. Once you make the connection between the task and something that motivates you, your energy levels rise, and you're ready to take action.

CONCLUSION

Mastering the Art of Linking

The power of linking is one of the most effective tools for unlocking motivation. By connecting tasks to things that matter to you, whether it's pleasure, importance, or certainty, you can transform even the most difficult or boring tasks into something you want to do. Linking allows you to tap into your internal Motivation Force and use it to accomplish anything.

Remember, linking isn't about forcing yourself to do something you don't want to do. It's about finding the natural connections between a task and the things that already motivate you. When you master the art of linking, you'll find that staying motivated becomes easier and more enjoyable. With practice, you can use this powerful tool to reach your goals and take control of your life.

Now let's look at how to use linking to tap into our greatest motivation drivers—and help us get any job done.

PART 2

THE MOTIVATION STACK

MAKE IT MEANINGFUL

Tapping Into Our Importance Drivers

IN 1951, 14-year-old James Harrison lay in a hospital bed in Australia, recovering from a major chest surgery. He'd lost one of his lungs. The operation saved his life, but only because of something invisible, silent, and powerful: a blood transfusion from a stranger.

That blood, and the donor behind it, saved James' life.

As James recovered, he made a quiet promise to himself:

"When I'm old enough, I'll become a blood donor."

Four years later, he kept that promise.

But what no one expected was this: James' blood wasn't just helpful—
it was extraordinary. Doctors discovered his blood contained a rare
antibody that could prevent Rh incompatibility, a dangerous condition
where a mother's blood attacks her unborn baby's blood cells.

This condition used to cause thousands of stillbirths every year.

But James' blood could stop it.

So doctors used it to develop a life-saving injection called Anti-D,
and they asked James to keep donating.

And he did. Every few weeks.

For more than 60 years.

He donated 1,173 times, saving over 2.4 million babies.

Parents all across Australia owe their children's lives to James Harrison.

And James? He never saw himself as a hero. He just saw it as his duty.

When asked why he never stopped, he simply said:

"My blood helped save someone once. That made it meaningful.
That made it me."

This chapter is about that same power.

When you connect what you have to do with who you are or who you want to be—even the hardest task becomes a holy mission.

WANT MOTIVATION? MAKE IT MEANINGFUL

We've already talked about how motivation comes from linking tasks to things that matter to us. One of the strongest ways to do this is by making tasks more meaningful.

In this chapter, we'll explore how to tap into what really matters to you—your *importance drivers*—and use them to get even the toughest tasks done.

Importance drivers are the things that you value most in life. They include your sense of purpose, your identity, and your values. When a task lines up with these drivers, it doesn't feel like a chore. Instead, it feels like something you want to do because it's part of who you are and what you believe in. Once you know how to connect your tasks to these drivers, you'll find that you have all the motivation you need to get them done.

WHY MEANING MATTERS

Think about a time when you felt highly motivated to do something. Chances are, it was something that had a lot of meaning to you. Maybe it was an important goal you wanted to achieve, or maybe it was something that reflected your values. The more meaningful a task feels, the more energy and focus you bring to it.

On the other hand, when something doesn't feel meaningful, it's easy to procrastinate. Tasks that seem pointless or unimportant are the ones we avoid, even if they need to be done. That's why it's so important to find ways to make every task meaningful. When we do, the task becomes more than just something to check off our to-do list—it becomes a way to live out our values and purpose.

For example, let's say you have to prepare a presentation at work, but you're not excited about it. If you see it as just another task, it's easy to put it off. But if you connect it to your bigger mission—like advancing in your career or showing your team that you're reliable—the task becomes more meaningful. Now, it feels important, and that gives you the motivation to get started.

TAPPING INTO YOUR PURPOSE

One of the strongest importance drivers is your sense of purpose. Purpose is the reason you do what you do. It's the thing that gives your life direction and makes you feel like you're working toward something bigger than yourself. When a task is linked to your purpose, it becomes more than just a chore—it becomes a step toward fulfilling your life's mission.

To tap into your purpose, here is a question you can ask:

 "How does this task help me move closer to my life goals?"

For example, if you're working on a project at work, think about how completing it will help you reach your long-term career goals. Or if you're struggling to keep up with a new habit, like exercising, connect it to your purpose of living a healthy, balanced life. When you see how the task fits into your bigger picture, it becomes easier to stay motivated.

Let's say your purpose is to be a good role model for your children. If you have to do something boring, like organizing your finances, think about how doing this will show your kids the importance of responsibility. Suddenly, the task has more meaning because it's tied to your purpose. This connection makes it easier to find the motivation to get it done.

LINKING TASKS TO YOUR IDENTITY

Another powerful importance driver is your identity—who you believe you are. Your identity is made up of the beliefs you hold about yourself and how you see yourself in the world. When a task is connected to your identity, it feels natural to do it, because it's in line with who you believe you are.

For example, if you see yourself as a responsible person, you're more likely to do things that reflect that identity, like paying your bills on time or keeping your commitments. On the other hand, if a task feels like it doesn't match who you are, it's harder to find the motivation to do it.

To tap into your identity, ask yourself:

 "How does this task help confirm what I believe about myself?"

For example, if you see yourself as someone who values health, you can link that identity to the task of exercising regularly. If you see yourself as someone who is hardworking, you can connect that to the tasks you do at work. By linking tasks to your identity, you're not just doing them because you "have to"—you're doing them because they're part of who you are.

Let's say you have to wake up early for a meeting, but you're struggling to get out of bed. If you remind yourself that you are someone who is disciplined and committed, it becomes easier to get up and get ready. The task feels like it aligns with your identity, and that makes it easier to follow through.

CONNECTING TASKS TO YOUR VALUES

Your values are the principles you believe in and stand for. They guide your decisions and actions, and they help you understand what's important in life. When a task is linked to your values, it feels meaningful because it's in line with what you believe.

For example, if one of your values is helping others, you can connect that value to tasks like volunteering or supporting your friends and family. If you value honesty, you'll be motivated to complete tasks that require integrity, like being transparent in your work or keeping your promises. The more a task aligns with your values, the more motivated you'll be to do it.

To tap into your values, ask yourself:

 "How does completing this task fulfill my highest values and what I stand for?"

For example, if you value self-improvement, you can link that value to tasks like reading, learning new skills, or setting personal goals. Or if you value family, you can connect that to spending quality time with your loved ones or taking care of household chores and responsibilities. When you see the connection between the task and your values, it feels more meaningful, and your motivation grows.

Let's say one of your values is being reliable. If you have a deadline approaching, you can remind yourself that completing the task on time reflects your value of being dependable. This link gives the task more meaning, and you're more likely to get it done without procrastinating.

EXERCISES TO MAKE TASKS MORE MEANINGFUL

Now that you know how to tap into your purpose, identity, and values, let's look at some simple exercises to make your tasks more meaningful. These exercises help you create strong links between the tasks you need to do and your importance drivers, so you can stay motivated.

EXERCISE 1: PURPOSE LINKING

1. Start by thinking of a task that you need to do but don't feel motivated to complete.
2. Now, ask yourself, "How will completing this task bring me closer to my purpose?"
3. List three to five ways the task connects to your bigger goals.
4. After making these connections, test your motivation by asking yourself how motivated you are to complete the task now.

Chances are, the task feels more important, and you're ready to get started.

EXERCISE 2: IDENTITY LINKING

1. Choose a task that you've been avoiding.
2. Ask yourself, "How does completing this task confirm what I believe about myself?"
3. List three to five reasons why this task reflects your identity.
4. Test your motivation level again.

When the task is linked to who you are, it feels more natural to get it done.

EXERCISE 3: VALUES LINKING

1. Pick a task that feels difficult or boring.
2. Ask yourself, "How does this task help me live out my values?"
3. List three to five ways the task connects to your core beliefs.
4. Once you've made the link, test your motivation level.

You'll likely find that the task now feels more meaningful and less like a chore.

These exercises are simple but powerful. By making the connection between the task and your purpose, identity, or values, you bring more meaning to what you're doing. This added meaning increases your motivation and helps you get things done with less resistance.

THE POWER OF SMALL WINS

As you work on making tasks more meaningful, remember to celebrate small wins along the way. Each time you complete a task that's linked to your importance drivers, take a moment to recognize your progress. These small victories build momentum and make it easier to stay motivated in the future.

For example, if you've been working on a big project at work and you've linked it to your purpose of growing in your career, celebrate each step you complete. Whether it's finishing a report, meeting a deadline, or getting positive feedback, every small win is a sign that you're moving closer to your goals. These small wins keep you energized, focused on the bigger picture and ultimately tip the Motivation Seesaw in your favor.

CONCLUSION

Living With Meaning and Motivation

When we make tasks meaningful, we tap into a deeper source of motivation. By linking what we need to do with our purpose, identity, and values, we transform everyday tasks into steps toward living a meaningful life. The more meaning we bring to our tasks, the easier it becomes to stay motivated and get things done.

Remember, motivation isn't about forcing yourself to do something you don't care about. It's about finding the connection between what you need to do and what really matters to you. When you master the art of making tasks meaningful, you'll find that staying motivated becomes a natural part of your life. Each task becomes a way to express who you are, live out your values, and move closer to your goals.

Now let's learn how to increase our motivation by making tasks more certain.

8

MAKE IT CERTAIN

Tapping Into Certainty Drivers

MOST PEOPLE WOULD never dream of climbing a 3,000-foot vertical rock face.

Even fewer would attempt it without sight.

But in 2017, Erik Weihenmayer, a blind adventurer, did exactly that.

With only the sound of a friend's voice guiding him through an earpiece, Erik scaled the nose of El Capitan, one of the most challenging rock faces in the world. Every inch he climbed required total trust—in his training, his equipment, his team, and most of all, himself.

At any point, uncertainty could have frozen him. A missed foothold. A misjudged grab. A moment of fear.

But Erik didn't stop.

Why?

Because he had built something stronger than fear:

Certainty.

Years earlier, Erik had already become the first blind person to reach the summit of Mount Everest. That success wasn't just a win—it was a deposit into his internal bank of belief. It gave him the confidence to tackle bigger, scarier challenges.

Each climb, each hard-earned foothold, each past success was a brick. And over time, those bricks built a solid foundation of certainty he could stand on, even in the dark.

That's what this chapter is about.

When you feel sure you can win, you'll begin, even if the odds are against you.

And every small victory becomes proof that you can go further than you ever imagined.

Let's learn how to build that kind of unshakable certainty—one brick at a time.

THE POWER OF CERTAINTY

We've already talked about how important it is to find meaning in the tasks we do. But the other key to motivation that's just as important is *certainty*.

Certainty is the feeling of confidence that you can accomplish something. When we feel certain that we can succeed, we're much more likely to start and finish a task. On the other hand, when we feel uncertain or unsure, it's easy to avoid the task or give up before we even begin.

Certainty is a powerful motivator because it gives us the confidence we need to take action. If you've ever been nervous about starting something new, you know how uncertainty can make you hesitate. But when you're sure you can do something, even if it's hard, you're more willing to give it a try.

In this chapter, we'll look at how to build certainty and use it to fuel your motivation.

WHY CERTAINTY MATTERS

Certainty is important because it helps us move forward with confidence. When you know you can do something, you don't waste time doubting yourself. Instead, you dive in and take action.

Think about a time when you were sure you could accomplish something. Maybe it was a project at work, a hobby you enjoy, or even a conversation with a friend. Because you were confident, you didn't hesitate to get started. You felt sure of your abilities, and that certainty made the task feel easier. On the other hand, if you've ever faced a task where you weren't sure of the outcome, it probably felt harder to begin.

Let's say you're learning to cook a new recipe. If you've cooked similar dishes before, you feel so confident that you can handle it—you jump right in. But if it's a complicated recipe and you've never tried it before, you'll feel uncertain. That uncertainty can make the task feel more intimidating, and it might even stop you from starting at all. Certainty makes all the difference between taking action and feeling stuck.

BUILDING CERTAINTY FROM PAST SUCCESS

One of the best ways to build certainty is by looking at your past successes. When you remind yourself of the things you've accomplished before, you build confidence in your ability to succeed again. This is why it's so important to keep track of your wins, no matter how small they are. Every time you achieve something, it adds to your sense of certainty.

For example, if you've successfully completed a work project in the past, you can use that memory to build certainty for future projects. Remind yourself, "I've done this before, and I can do it again." This simple thought helps you feel more confident and ready to tackle the next task.

Even if the task is new, you can still look for similarities to things you've done before. Maybe you've never run a marathon, but you've trained for other physical challenges. You can use those past expe-riences to boost your certainty. You might say, "I've faced tough physical challenges before, so I know I can train for this marathon too." By linking new tasks to past successes, you make them feel more achievable.

BREAKING TASKS INTO SMALL STEPS

Another way to build certainty is by breaking big tasks into smaller, more manageable steps. When a task feels too big or overwhelming, it's easy to doubt yourself. But when you focus on just one small step at a time, it feels easier and less intimidating. Each small step you complete builds your confidence and makes the task seem more achievable. This step-by-step approach helps you avoid feeling overwhelmed, and as you accomplish each small part of the task, your certainty grows.

For example, if you need to write a long report, don't think about writing the entire thing all at once. Start by outlining the main points or writing the introduction. Once that small piece is done, you'll feel more confident about moving on to the next section. By focusing on completing one small part at a time, the whole task becomes much easier to manage, and your certainty in finishing the task increases.

This approach can be used for almost any goal. If you're trying to improve your fitness, start with short, simple workouts rather than overwhelming yourself with long routines. As you complete each small workout, your confidence will grow, and you'll feel more certain that you can reach your fitness goals.

LEARNING FROM OTHERS' SUCCESS

Sometimes, building certainty comes from looking at the successes of others. When you see that someone else has accomplished something similar to what you're trying to do, it can boost your belief that you can do it too. Seeing that someone else succeeded makes the goal feel more achievable.

For example, if you're trying to start your own business but feel uncertain about whether you can do it, look for stories of people who were in similar situations and succeeded. Read about how they overcame obstacles and what steps they took to reach their goals. Learning from their experiences can help you feel more confident and certain that you can follow a similar path.

Another way to learn from others is by talking to people who have already achieved what you're working toward. Ask them for advice, learn about their journey, and see how they handled the challenges along the way. This can give you valuable insights and make you feel more certain that you can succeed too.

VISUALIZING SUCCESS

Visualization is another powerful tool for building certainty. When you imagine yourself successfully completing a task, it helps boost your confidence and makes the goal feel more real. Visualization allows you to mentally practice the steps you need to take, which helps you feel more prepared and certain that you can accomplish the task.

For example, if you're preparing for a big presentation, take a few minutes to close your eyes and visualize yourself confidently delivering the presentation. Picture the audience responding positively, and imagine how good it will feel to finish the presentation successfully. This mental rehearsal helps reduce uncertainty and makes the task feel more manageable.

Visualization works because it tricks your brain into feeling like you've already experienced success. The more vividly you can imagine the steps and the outcome, the more certain you'll feel about your ability to make it happen in real life.

CELEBRATING SMALL WINS

Celebrating small wins is another great way to build certainty and keep your motivation high. Each time you complete a small step toward your goal, take a moment to recognize your progress. Celebrating these victories reminds you that you're capable of achieving your goals and gives you the confidence to keep going.

For example, if your goal is to write a book, celebrate each chapter you complete. Whether it's treating yourself to something special or simply taking a moment to reflect on your progress, acknowledging these small milestones helps build certainty that you can finish the whole book.

Celebrating small wins also helps you stay focused on the progress you've made, rather than worrying about how much more there is to do. It shifts your mindset from "I still have so far to go" to "I'm getting closer to my goal every day."

CONCLUSION

Using Certainty to Fuel Your Motivation

Certainty is a key driver of motivation. When you feel confident that you can accomplish something, it's much easier to take action and keep going. By building certainty through small steps, learning from past successes, visualizing the outcome, and celebrating small wins, you can make even the most daunting tasks feel achievable.

The more certain you feel about your ability to succeed, the less likely you are to procrastinate or give up. Certainty gives you the confidence to push through challenges and stay focused on your goals.

Remember, certainty isn't something that magically appears—it's something you build through practice and progress. The more you work on building your confidence and breaking tasks into manageable pieces, the stronger your Motivation Force will become. With certainty on your side, you can tackle any task, no matter how big or small.

Now let's learn the easiest motivation tactic of all, and how we can use it to get any task done.

9

MAKE IT EASY

Tapping Into the Avoidance of Pain Driver

AT JUST 22 YEARS OLD, Ali Truwit was a competitive swimmer at Yale with big dreams and a bright future ahead. But everything changed during a snorkeling trip in Turks and Caicos, when she was suddenly attacked by a shark. The brutal incident led to the amputation of her leg above the knee, leaving her physically and emotionally devastated. In the days that followed, Ali believed one thing for sure—she would never swim again.

But Ali didn't stay down.

Within a year of the attack, she found the courage to step back into the water. Not to float or relax—but to swim again. At first, her steps were small and slow. She began simply by standing in the water. Then she tried splashing around. Eventually, she pushed herself to take a few strokes using a prosthetic leg. She didn't aim for perfection—she just focused on one manageable step at a time.

Those small steps added up. Fast.

Today, Ali is a silver medalist for Team USA at the 2024 Paralympics, and she's currently training for the New York City Marathon. What once felt impossible is now part of her everyday life—not because she forced herself through pain, but because she started with one small step.

Ali could have given up—no one would have blamed her. Her trauma was intense and real. But she didn't try to leap back all at once. She made the path easier. One simple step at a time.

Now, in this chapter, we'll explore how you can do the same in your life. You don't have to take on everything at once. Just one small step can be the start of something powerful.

MAKE IT EASY

One of the strongest forces in human behavior is the desire to avoid pain. We naturally move away from things that feel hard, uncomfortable, or unpleasant. This instinct is built into us because, in the past, avoiding pain often meant survival.

However, in today's world, this instinct can get in the way of our goals. Tasks that feel difficult or uncomfortable are often the ones we avoid, even though completing them would help us in the long run.

In this chapter, we'll explore how to make tasks feel easier by tapping into our natural desire to avoid pain. When we make a task easier, we reduce the pain associated with it. This makes it more likely that we'll actually do the task, instead of avoiding it. We'll also look at some strategies for making even the hardest tasks feel less overwhelming.

WHY WE AVOID HARD TASKS

Avoiding hard or uncomfortable tasks is something we all do. It's not because we're lazy; it's because our brains are wired to avoid pain. If a task feels too difficult, stressful, or boring, we're more likely to put it off. Our brains would rather do something that feels easy and pleasurable in the moment, like watching TV or scrolling through social media.

Imagine you have a big project due at work, but every time you sit down to start it, it feels overwhelming. Your brain starts looking for an escape. Instead of working on the project, you decide to check your email or clean your desk. These small distractions feel easier, so your brain chooses them to avoid the discomfort of starting the project.

The problem with avoiding hard tasks is that it doesn't make them go away. In fact, avoiding them often makes things worse. The longer we put off a task, the more stress and guilt we feel. That's why it's important to find ways to make hard tasks feel easier. When we reduce the pain, we reduce the urge to avoid them.

HOW TO MAKE TASKS EASIER

One of the best ways to make tasks feel easier is to break them down into smaller steps. When a task feels too big, it's easy to get overwhelmed. But when you focus on just one small part of the task, it feels more manageable. Each small step you complete gives you a sense of accomplishment, which makes the next step feel easier.

For example, let's say you need to clean your entire house, but the thought of doing it all at once feels overwhelming. Instead of trying to tackle the whole house, break it down into smaller tasks. Start with just one room, or even just one part of a room, like your bed. Once you've completed that small step, you'll feel more motivated to keep going. By breaking the task into smaller pieces, you make it feel less painful.

USE A TIMER TO GET STARTED

Another way to make tasks easier is to set a timer and commit to working on the task for just a few minutes. Often, the hardest part of any task is getting started. Once you begin, you'll find it easier to keep going. By setting a short time limit, you remove the pressure of having to finish the whole task, and instead focus on making progress.

For example, if you're dreading starting a big project, set a timer for just 5 or 10 minutes. Tell yourself you only need to work on it for that short period of time. Once the timer goes off, you can decide whether to stop or keep going. Most of the time, you'll find that getting started was the hardest part, and once you've begun, you'll want to keep working.

Using a timer makes the task feel more manageable because you're not committing to hours of work—just a few minutes. It's a great way to trick your brain into starting without feeling overwhelmed.

THE POWER OF SIMPLICITY

Simplicity is another tool we can use to make tasks feel easier. When a task feels complicated, it's easy to get stuck. Our brains don't like dealing with too many choices or steps at once. By simplifying the task, we remove the mental barriers that make it feel difficult.

For example, if you're trying to start a new exercise routine, don't make it complicated. You don't need a perfect workout plan or fancy equipment. Just start with something simple, like walking for 10 minutes a day. Once you've built the habit, you can add more complexity later. By keeping it simple, you make it easier to get started and stick with it.

Simplicity also helps reduce decision fatigue. When we have too many options or decisions to make, it's easy to get overwhelmed and do nothing. By simplifying tasks, we remove the need to make a lot of decisions, which makes it easier to take action. For example, if you're trying to eat healthier, don't overwhelm yourself with a complicated meal plan. Start by simplifying your meals—choose a few healthy options and stick with them. The fewer decisions you have to make, the easier it becomes to follow through.

CHANGE YOUR ENVIRONMENT

Your environment has a big impact on how easy or hard a task feels. Sometimes, simply changing where you work or adjusting your surroundings can make a task feel easier. If you're stuck or unmotivated, take a look at your environment and make small changes that can help you focus.

For example, if you're trying to work on a project but your desk is cluttered, spend a few minutes cleaning it up. A clean, organized space can help you feel more in control and less overwhelmed. If you're feeling distracted by noise, try moving to a quieter location or using noise-canceling headphones. Sometimes, even small changes like opening a window or sitting in a different chair can help refresh your mind and make the task feel more approachable.

Changing your environment is a simple way to reduce the pain associated with starting a task. It can help you feel more focused and ready to take on the challenge.

USE VISUAL CUES TO STAY ON TRACK

Visual cues can help make tasks easier by reminding you of what needs to be done and helping you stay focused. A simple to-do list, a calendar, or even sticky notes can serve as visual reminders that keep you on track. These cues help you organize your tasks and reduce the mental effort of remembering everything you need to do.

For example, if you're working on a big project, break it down into smaller tasks and write each one on a sticky note. As you complete each task, remove the note from your board. This gives you a clear visual representation of your progress and helps you stay motivated to keep going.

You can also use visual cues to remind yourself of the next small step in a task. For example, if you're writing a report, keep a checklist of sections you need to complete. Having this list in front of you helps reduce the mental load of figuring out what to do next, making the task feel more manageable.

ELIMINATE UNNECESSARY STEPS

Sometimes, tasks feel hard because we make them more complicated than they need to be. Take a moment to review the task and see if there are any steps you can eliminate or simplify. By removing unnecessary steps, you reduce the effort required to complete the task, making it easier to get started.

For example, if you're preparing a presentation and feel overwhelmed by all the information you need to include, ask yourself if there are any details that aren't essential. Simplifying the presentation by focusing on the key points makes the task easier and reduces the time it will take to finish.

This approach applies to many areas of life. Whether it's simplifying your morning routine, streamlining your work processes, or cutting out unnecessary steps in a project, eliminating complexity helps make tasks easier and less painful.

CONCLUSION

Making Tasks Easier to Reduce Pain

Our natural instinct is to avoid pain, and that's why we often put off tasks that feel difficult or uncomfortable. But by using strategies that make tasks easier—like breaking them into smaller steps, using a timer, changing your environment, and simplifying the process—we reduce the pain and increase the likelihood of getting things done.

Remember, making tasks easier isn't about avoiding responsibility—it's about removing the mental and physical barriers that hold us back from taking action. The easier a task feels, the less likely we are to avoid it, and the more likely we are to stay motivated and focused. By applying these strategies, you can make even the toughest tasks feel more manageable and reduce the urge to procrastinate.

Now let's learn about how to increase our motivation by tapping into our deep human need to have some fun.

10

MAKE IT FUN, INTERESTING, EXCITING, AND SATISFYING

Tapping Into Pleasure Drivers

WHEN MATT FRAZIER started training for his first marathon, he wasn't an athlete. He wasn't even healthy. Like many people, he struggled to stay consistent with exercise. Every long run felt like torture. He hated waking up early. He hated the sore muscles. He hated how boring it all felt.

Until one day, something clicked.

He realized he didn't have to suffer through his workouts—he could gamify them. He could make running fun.

He started listening to music that fired him up. He gave himself little rewards after each training session—a smoothie, a funny podcast, a favorite movie. He tracked his progress on an app that turned each mile into a mini victory. He joined online running forums where he could celebrate his small wins with others.

Suddenly, he wasn't forcing himself to train anymore, he wanted to. The pain didn't go away, but it got pushed to the side by something stronger: pleasure.

Matt didn't just finish his marathon. He went on to become an ultra-marathoner, running races over 50 miles long,

"When I stopped making running a punishment, and started making it fun... everything changed."

When we add pleasure to pain, tasks go from dreadful to doable. When we inject fun, curiosity, and satisfaction into the things we resist, motivation becomes natural.

This chapter will show how to turn your boring tasks into enjoyable ones—and make progress feel like play.

THE POWER OF FUN

We've already talked about how avoiding pain can motivate us to get things done. But there's another powerful force that can drive our actions: *pleasure*. When something is fun, interesting, or exciting, we're naturally drawn to it. This is why we often find it easier to spend hours on activities we enjoy, while we struggle to motivate ourselves for things that feel boring or difficult. The good news is we can use the power of pleasure to make even the hardest tasks more enjoyable.

In this chapter, we'll explore how to tap into your pleasure drivers to stay motivated. When you make tasks fun, interesting, and satisfying, they stop feeling like a chore. Instead, they become something you look forward to. We'll look at how to turn boring tasks into something enjoyable, how to add excitement to your work, and how to create a sense of satisfaction in everything you do.

WHY FUN MATTERS

Think about a time when you did something just because it was fun. Maybe it was a hobby, a sport, or even a game. You probably didn't need anyone to push you to do it. The fun and interest in the activity were enough to keep you going. This is the power of pleasure—it motivates us to take action without needing to force ourselves.

But what happens when a task doesn't seem fun or interesting? We often avoid it. Whether it's a boring report, a repetitive task, or something that feels unimportant, it's hard to stay motivated when the task lacks pleasure. That's why we need to find ways to add fun and interest to the things we don't naturally enjoy.

For example, if you have to write a long report for work, you might dread the idea of sitting down for hours and typing. But if you add something fun, like listening to your favorite music while you work, the task becomes more enjoyable. Suddenly, the report doesn't seem as boring, and you're more motivated to get it done. When you combine something enjoyable with the task, it becomes easier to stay focused and energized.

MAKING EVEN THE MOST BORING TASKS FUN

One of the simplest ways to make a task more enjoyable is to add a fun element to it. This doesn't mean you need to turn every task into a party, but even small changes can make a big difference. For example, if you're doing housework, you could dance to upbeat music so that it makes you feel energized. If you're working on a big project, you could take short breaks to do something you enjoy, like going for a walk or grabbing your favorite snack.

Another way to make tasks more fun is to turn them into gamify them. For example, you could challenge yourself to complete a task in a certain amount of time, like racing against the clock. Or you could create a points system where you reward yourself for completing small steps of a task. Gamifying a task adds an element of excitement, and it helps take your mind off the hard parts.

Let's say you need to clean your garage, but it feels like a boring and overwhelming job. Instead of just focusing on the end result, break it down into smaller tasks and reward yourself for each step you complete. Maybe after cleaning one section, you treat yourself to a cold drink, a piece of chocolate or a short break to watch funny YouTube videos. By adding these fun rewards, you make the task more interesting and easier to finish.

Another way to make a task more enjoyable is to do it with someone else. If you're working on a project or doing a difficult task, having a friend or coworker join you can make it feel less like work and more like a shared experience. You'll feel more motivated because you're not doing it alone.

MAKE TASKS INTERESTING BY LEARNING SOMETHING NEW

Sometimes, a task feels boring because it doesn't challenge us or teach us anything new. One way to overcome this is by finding a way to learn something from the task. When we're learning, we feel more engaged, and the task becomes more interesting.

For example, if you have a repetitive task at work, like entering data into a spreadsheet, you could challenge yourself to learn a new shortcut or tool that makes the task faster. By focusing on improving your skills, the task becomes a learning experience, rather than just something boring to get through. The more you learn, the more interesting the task feels, and the easier it is to stay motivated.

You can also make tasks more interesting by changing how you approach them. For example, if you're working on a long-term project, try looking at it from a different perspective. Ask yourself, "How can

I do this task better than I've ever done it before?" This approach adds a layer of challenge and curiosity to the task, making it feel more interesting. You might discover new ways to be more efficient, creative, or effective. By treating the task as a chance to grow and improve, you stay engaged and motivated to see it through.

For example, let's say you're working on organizing files at your job. Instead of seeing it as a boring task, ask yourself how you can improve the system to make it more efficient. Could you develop a new method for categorizing files? Could you use a software tool to automate parts of the process? By turning the task into an opportunity to learn and improve, you make it more stimulating and rewarding.

THE POWER OF EXCITEMENT

Excitement is a powerful motivator. When we feel excited about something, we're more likely to dive in and take action. The key to using excitement as a motivation tool is to create it, even when it doesn't come naturally. You can do this by focusing on the positive outcomes of the task and the benefits that come with completing it.

For example, let's say you need to start a new fitness routine, but you're not feeling excited about it. One way to create excitement is to visualize the results you want to achieve. Imagine how strong and healthy you'll feel after sticking to your routine for a few weeks. Picture yourself reaching your fitness goals, whether it's running a race, losing weight, or gaining more energy. By focusing on the exciting outcomes, you'll feel more motivated to get started.

Another way to build excitement is to set a challenge for yourself. Challenges create a sense of urgency and make the task feel more thrilling. For example, if you're working on a project, challenge yourself to complete it ahead of schedule or with extra creativity. The excitement of the challenge makes the task feel more engaging and less like a burden.

CREATING A SENSE OF SATISFACTION

While fun and excitement can help us start a task, *satisfaction* is what keeps us going. Satisfaction comes from knowing that what we're doing is meaningful and that we're making progress. It's that feeling of accomplishment we get when we complete something important.

One way to create satisfaction is to celebrate small wins along the way. If you're working on a long-term goal, break it into smaller milestones and reward yourself each time you reach one. These small moments of success give you the satisfaction of knowing you're moving in the right direction. They keep you motivated to continue working toward your bigger goal.

For example, if you're writing a book, don't wait until the whole book is finished to feel satisfied. Instead, celebrate each chapter you complete. Give yourself a reward, like posting your success on social media and getting encouragement from family and friends. Or buy yourself a delicious lunch for each chapter you finish. By acknowledging your progress, you create a sense of satisfaction that keeps you motivated to finish the entire project.

Another way to create satisfaction is to focus on the impact of your work. Ask yourself, "Who will benefit from what I'm doing?" Whether it's your family, your coworkers, or your community, knowing that your efforts are making a difference can give you a deep sense of fulfillment. When we see the positive results of our work, it feels satisfying, and we're more likely to stay motivated.

MAKING TASKS REWARDING

To tap into your pleasure drivers, it's important to find ways to make tasks rewarding. Rewards don't always have to be physical or material; they can be emotional too. Feeling proud of your work, seeing the results of your efforts, checking a box to acknowledge your completion of the task—or knowing that you're helping others can all be rewarding experiences.

For example, if you're volunteering for a community project, the reward might not be a paycheck, but the satisfaction of knowing you're making a difference. Or, if you're working on a creative project, the reward could be the joy of expressing yourself and sharing your ideas with others. By focusing on the emotional rewards of a task, you can make it feel more meaningful and enjoyable.

It's also helpful to create a reward system for yourself. For example, after completing a difficult task, treat yourself to something you enjoy, like a relaxing evening or a special treat. These small rewards help make the task feel more pleasurable and give you something to look forward to.

CONCLUSION

Making Tasks Fun, Exciting, and Satisfying

When we add fun, interest, excitement, and satisfaction to our tasks, they stop feeling like chores and become something we want to do. By tapping into our pleasure drivers, we can turn even the most boring or difficult tasks into something enjoyable and rewarding.

The key is to find what works for you. Whether it's adding a fun element, learning something new, setting exciting challenges, or celebrating small wins, you can use these strategies to make tasks feel more engaging. When you make tasks fun and satisfying, motivation comes naturally, and you'll find it easier to reach your goals.

Now let's learn how to combine all of these motivation techniques to create an unstoppable force, to help you get anything done.

11

IGNITE THE FIRE

Combining Your Motivation Drivers

NOW THAT WE'VE explored the different drivers of motivation—pleasure, pain, importance, and certainty—it's time to put them all together. When you combine these forces, you create a powerful boost in motivation that can help you accomplish anything. It's like building a fire. Each driver of motivation is like adding fuel, and when they come together, they ignite a fire that pushes you forward. In this chapter, we'll learn how to combine these drivers and use them to fuel your motivation for any task, no matter how challenging.

When we focus on just one driver, like avoiding pain or seeking pleasure, we can still get things done. But when we add in the other drivers, like making the task feel important and adding certainty that we can do it, our motivation skyrockets. This combination makes us feel unstoppable and ready to take on even the hardest challenges.

STARTING WITH MEANING AND PURPOSE

The first step in igniting your motivation fire is to start with meaning and purpose. We've already talked about how making a task meaningful can boost your motivation. When something is connected to your deeper goals or values, it feels important, and that importance gives you energy to get it done. But meaning alone isn't always enough. To create a strong fire of motivation, we need to add more fuel.

Let's say you're working on a big project at work, and you know it's important because it will help your team succeed. That sense of purpose is a great start. But to really ignite your motivation, you need to combine that meaning with other drivers, like pleasure and the avoidance of pain. When all of these forces come together, you'll find that the project doesn't just feel important—it feels exciting and achievable too.

ADDING THE PLEASURE AND PAIN DRIVERS

Once you've connected a task to your purpose, the next step is to tap into your pleasure and pain drivers. This means focusing on the rewards of completing the task and the consequences of not doing it. When we focus on pleasure and pain together, we create a powerful push-and-pull effect that drives us to take action.

For example, if you're trying to start a new exercise routine, think about the pleasure you'll get from feeling stronger, healthier, and more energetic. Imagine how good it will feel to reach your fitness goals. At the same time, consider the pain of not exercising—feeling tired, out of shape, or unhealthy in the long run. By focusing on both the positive and negative outcomes, you're giving yourself two strong reasons to get started.

The pleasure and pain drivers are like two sides of a seesaw. When you add enough weight to the pleasure side (the benefits of completing the task) and the reduce the weight on the pain side (by reflecting on the consequences of avoiding it), the seesaw tips in your favor. This combination creates a strong urge to take action because you want to avoid the pain and enjoy the pleasure at the same time.

BUILDING CERTAINTY

After you've tapped into meaning, pleasure, and pain, the next step is to build certainty. Certainty gives you confidence that you can succeed. When you feel sure that you can complete a task, it feels less overwhelming, and you're more likely to take action. Certainty acts like a steady flame that keeps your motivation fire burning.

Think about times when you've accomplished something similar before. Remind yourself, "I've done this before, and I can do it again." This simple thought helps you feel more confident and ready to tackle the next task.

Also, build your certainty by breaking the task into smaller steps. Instead of looking at the whole project and feeling overwhelmed, focus on just the first step. Each small step you complete gives you more confidence that you can finish the task. This sense of progress helps build momentum, and before you know it, the task starts to feel more doable.

CREATING A PLAN

Now that you've combined meaning, pleasure, pain, and certainty, the next step is to create a plan. Having a clear plan makes the task feel more structured and less overwhelming. It also helps you stay on track and measure your progress. A good plan includes small, achievable steps that lead you toward your goal.

For example, if you're working on a big project, break it down and create a timeline for when each task needs to be completed. This not only helps you stay organized, but it also makes the project feel more manageable. Each time you complete a step in your plan, you'll feel a sense of accomplishment, which keeps your motivation fire burning.

Creating a plan also helps you stay focused on the task at hand. When you know exactly what needs to be done and when, you're less likely to get distracted or overwhelmed. A clear plan gives you direction, and that direction fuels your motivation to keep going.

MAKING IT REWARDING AND SATISFYING

Rewards are a powerful way to fuel your motivation fire. When you know there's a reward waiting for you at the end of a task, it gives you something to look forward to. But rewards don't have to be big or complicated. They can be small and simple, like treating yourself to a snack, taking a break, or doing something you enjoy after completing a task.

For example, if you've been working hard on a project, reward yourself with a break to watch your favorite show or take a relaxing walk outside. These small rewards help make the process more satisfying and give you the pleasure of knowing that your hard work is paying off.

Satisfaction also comes from seeing the impact of your efforts. When you complete a task, take a moment to appreciate the difference it made. Whether it's cleaning your house, finishing a report, or reaching a fitness goal, acknowledging your success helps build a sense of accomplishment. This feeling of satisfaction keeps your motivation fire burning and makes you want to keep going.

MAINTAINING MOMENTUM

One of the biggest challenges with motivation is keeping it going over time. It's easy to feel motivated at the start of a project, but as the days or weeks go on, that motivation can fade. That's why it's important to maintain momentum. Momentum is like adding logs to the fire—each log keeps the fire burning, and the more you add, the stronger the fire becomes.

To maintain momentum, focus on small wins. Each time you complete a task or reach a milestone, take a moment to celebrate your progress. This doesn't mean you need to throw a party, but giving yourself a small reward or acknowledging your success can help keep you motivated. These small wins act like fuel that keeps your motivation fire going.

Another way to maintain momentum is to remember to stay connected to your purpose. Remind yourself regularly why the task is important and how it aligns with your bigger goals. This helps you stay focused on the meaning behind the task, even when it feels challenging. The more you stay connected to your purpose, the easier it is to keep going.

OVERCOMING OBSTACLES

No matter how motivated you are, obstacles are bound to come up. When they do, it's important not to let them extinguish your motivation fire. Instead, think of obstacles as opportunities to strengthen your motivation. Each time you overcome an obstacle, you build more confidence in your ability to succeed.

One way to overcome obstacles is to stay flexible. If your original plan isn't working, be willing to adjust it. This doesn't mean giving up on your goal—it just means finding a new path to get there. Flexibility helps you stay focused on the end result, even when things don't go as planned.

Another strategy for overcoming obstacles is to ask for help. Sometimes, all it takes is a fresh perspective or a little support to get back on track. Whether it's talking to a coworker, friend, or mentor, getting help can reignite your motivation and help you push through any challenges.

REIGNITING YOUR MOTIVATION WHEN IT FADES

There will be times when your motivation fire starts to fade. Maybe you've hit a rough patch, or maybe you're feeling tired and discouraged. When this happens, it's important to reignite your motivation before it goes out completely. The good news is, you already have the tools to do this.

Start by reconnecting with your purpose. Ask yourself why the task is important and how it aligns with your goals. Then, focus on the pleasure and pain drivers. Remind yourself of the rewards you'll get from completing the task and the consequences of not doing it. Finally, build certainty by reviewing your past successes and breaking the task up into smaller steps. By reigniting these drivers, you'll feel your motivation fire start to burn again.

CONCLUSION

The Power of Combining Motivation Drivers

When you combine the drivers of motivation—importance, pleasure, pain, certainty, and rewards—you create a powerful force that can help you accomplish anything. These drivers work together to fuel your motivation and keep you moving forward, even when the task feels difficult or overwhelming. By tapping into all of these forces—making tasks meaningful, fun, easy, rewarding, and satisfying—you can ignite a raging fire that pushes you to reach your goals with less resistance.

The key to staying motivated is not just waiting for inspiration or energy to strike. Instead, it's about actively creating the conditions that make motivation easier. When you make a task fun and easy, link it to your purpose, add the promise of rewards, and remind yourself of past successes, you'll find that motivation comes naturally. You don't have to struggle to stay on track because you've built an environment where you're excited to keep going.

Remember, motivation isn't something that appears by magic—it's something you can create by combining these powerful drivers. Whether it's for a big project at work, a personal goal, or even everyday tasks, you now have the tools to light your motivation fire. With this combination of forces working for you, you'll be able to take on any challenge and keep moving forward, even when it gets tough.

The more you practice combining these motivation drivers, the easier it becomes to stay motivated in all areas of your life. You'll notice that tasks feel less like chores and more like opportunities to grow, succeed, and enjoy the process. By making tasks fun, easy, rewarding, and meaningful, you're not just getting things done—you're creating a life filled with energy, progress, and satisfaction. This is the power of igniting the Motivation Force, and now, you know how to keep it burning strong.

PART 3

THE
MOTIVATED
LIFE

12

HACKS TO GET MOTIVATED QUICKLY

TARYN WIESE WAS a 31-year-old mom from Iowa. She had a happy life, a loving husband, and two small kids. Life felt full and simple—until one icy winter day.

She was driving with her children when a large truck ran a red light and smashed into their car. Her kids survived with only a few cuts. But Taryn? She was crushed.

Her injuries were so bad that doctors had to amputate her leg above the knee. She woke up in a hospital bed, surrounded by wires, beeping machines, and the crushing news:

"You'll never walk again the same way."

Taryn was heartbroken. She couldn't imagine chasing her kids around the yard, dancing in the kitchen, or even standing long enough to make breakfast.

But then she made a choice.

Not a loud, bold choice. A quiet one:

"I'll just try to stand today."

It was hard. Painful. Slow.

But standing turned into taking a step with a walker.

Then a second.

Then a third.

And six months later, she walked across her kitchen, holding her daughter's hand.

She said, "I didn't start with courage. I found it after I moved."

Today, she uses a prosthetic leg and walks proudly. She even speaks at schools, telling kids, "You don't need to feel brave to get started. You just need to move."

YOU JUST NEED TO MOVE

There are times when we need motivation right away. Maybe we've been putting off a task for too long, or maybe we just feel stuck and need a boost. Whatever the case, finding ways to get motivated fast is important for staying on track.

In this chapter, we'll explore some quick hacks that can help you find motivation when you need it most. These hacks don't take a lot of time, but they can make a big difference when you're feeling unmotivated or overwhelmed.

THE POWER OF THE 5-SECOND RULE

One of the easiest and most effective hacks for getting motivated fast is the 5-second rule made famous by Mel Robbins. This rule is simple: when you have an idea to do something, you count down from five—"5, 4, 3, 2, 1"—and then act on it before your brain talks you out of it. This quick countdown stops you from over-thinking or procrastinating. By the time you hit "1," you've already started moving.

The reason this works is that it stops the hesitation that often keeps us stuck. When you give yourself too much time to think, your brain starts coming up with reasons to avoid the task. But when you count down and act immediately, you bypass that resistance. It's a simple trick, but it's powerful because it gets you moving right away.

For example, let's say you've been putting off starting a workout. You know you should get up and do it, but you keep finding reasons to delay. Instead of letting your brain take over with excuses, use the 5-second rule. Count down—"5, 4, 3, 2, 1"—and then get up and start. Once you've started, you'll find it easier to keep going.

THE 2-MINUTE RULE

Another great hack for quick motivation is the 2-minute rule. The 2-minute rule is one of the simplest and most effective hacks for staying motivated and productive.

This rule says that if something will take two minutes or less to complete, do it right away. The idea is that small tasks can pile up and become overwhelming if we let them sit for too long. But if a task can be done in just a couple of minutes, there's no reason to put it off.

Think about all the small tasks that come up throughout the day— taking out the garbage, sweeping the floor, sending a quick email, responding to a message, or putting away some dishes. These tasks don't take much time, but we often delay doing them because they feel like minor interruptions. The problem is, when these little tasks pile up, they can make us feel stressed or overwhelmed.

The 2-minute rule is a way to prevent these small tasks from building up. By committing to handling anything that takes two minutes or less immediately, you clear them off your to-do list and free up mental space for the bigger tasks that require more focus.

For example, if you notice the trash is full and you know it'll only take two minutes to take it out, just do it. If you need to send a quick email reply, don't wait—just send it. By handling these small tasks right away, you avoid creating a backlog of tiny chores that can become a burden later.

The 2-minute rule also helps you build momentum. When you start completing small tasks quickly, you feel a sense of accomplishment, which can motivate you to tackle the bigger tasks on your list. It's a simple but powerful way to stay on top of your responsibilities and avoid procrastination.

THE 5-MINUTE RULE

The 5-minute rule is a great way to overcome the hardest part of any task: getting started. Often, when we think about a project or chore, it seems overwhelming, and we don't know where to begin. This can make us procrastinate, putting off tasks we know we need to do. The 5-minute rule helps you break through this resistance by committing to work on the task for just five minutes.

The idea is simple: promise yourself that you'll only work on the task for five minutes, and then you can stop if you want. Five minutes doesn't feel like a big commitment, so it's easier to get started. But here's the trick: once you've started, you'll often find that the task isn't as bad as you thought, and you'll want to keep going. The momentum you create in those five minutes can carry you through the rest of the task.

For example, let's say you need to write a report for work, but the thought of sitting down and writing the whole thing feels overwhelming. Instead of thinking about the entire project, just commit to writing for five minutes. Once you've written for those five minutes, you'll probably feel more comfortable continuing because the hardest part—starting—is already behind you. Even if you don't finish the entire report in one sitting, you've made progress, and that's what matters.

The 5-minute rule works because it reduces the mental barrier to getting started. By focusing on a small, manageable amount of time, you trick your brain into taking action. Once you've begun, you often realize that the task isn't as difficult or time-consuming as you feared, and that's when the real progress begins.

CHANGE YOUR ENVIRONMENT

Sometimes, getting motivated is as simple as changing your environment. Your surroundings have a big impact on how you feel, and making small adjustments to your space can help boost your motivation. If you're feeling unmotivated, take a moment to look around. Is your space cluttered? Is it full of distractions? If so, a quick change might be all you need to get moving.

For example, if you're trying to work but keep getting distracted by your phone, move your phone to another room or put it on silent. If your desk is messy, take a few minutes to tidy it up. A clean, organized space can make you feel more focused and ready to tackle the task at hand. Sometimes, even moving to a different room or sitting by a window can give you a fresh perspective and new energy.

Changing your environment isn't just about removing distractions, it's also about adding things that inspire you. If music helps you focus, put on your favorite playlist. If fresh air helps clear your mind, open a window or step outside for a few minutes. These small changes can have a big impact on your mood and motivation.

VISUALIZE SUCCESS

Visualization is a powerful tool for getting motivated quickly. When you picture yourself succeeding, it gives you a boost of confidence and excitement. It also helps you focus on the positive outcome of the task, rather than the difficulty of starting it. By visualizing success, you create a mental image of what it will feel like to accomplish your goal, which makes it easier to take action.

To use this hack, take a few moments to close your eyes and imagine yourself completing the task you're avoiding. Picture yourself feeling proud and satisfied with the result. Imagine how relieved and happy you'll feel once it's done. This simple visualization helps shift your focus from the difficulty of the task to the positive feelings that come from finishing it.

For example, if you need to write a report but feel unmotivated, close your eyes and visualize yourself finishing it. Picture the sense of accomplishment you'll feel when it's done. Imagine yourself turning it in and feeling proud of your work. This mental picture can help spark the motivation you need to get started.

CREATE A REWARD SYSTEM

Rewards are a great way to boost motivation, especially when you're facing a tough or boring task. Knowing that there's something enjoyable waiting for you at the end can give you the push you need to get started. The key is to choose a reward that's meaningful to you, whether it's something small like a snack or something bigger like taking time off to relax.

The reward doesn't have to be big—it just needs to be something that makes you feel good. For example, if you've been putting off a task at work, promise yourself a short break or a coffee once it's done. If you need to complete a workout, reward yourself with a relaxing shower or a fun activity afterward. The anticipation of the reward makes the task feel less like a chore and more like something worth doing.

To make the reward system work even better, break larger tasks into smaller pieces and reward yourself for each step you complete. For example, if you're working on a big project, reward yourself for finishing each section or milestone. These small rewards help you stay motivated throughout the process, rather than just at the end.

CHANGE YOUR LANGUAGE

The way you talk to yourself can have a big impact on your motivation. If you're telling yourself, "I have to do this," it can make the task feel like a burden. But if you change your language to something more positive, like "I get to do this," it shifts your mindset and makes the task feel more like an opportunity than a chore.

For example, instead of saying, "I have to go to the gym," try saying, "I get to go to the gym and take care of my health." This small change in language helps you focus on the positive aspects of the task and makes you feel more grateful and motivated to do it. It's a simple mental shift, but it can have a big impact on how you feel about the task.

Another way to change your language is to focus on progress rather than perfection. Instead of saying, "I have to finish this project perfectly," say, "I'll make progress on this project today." This reduces the pressure and makes it easier to get started. When you're not focused on doing things perfectly, you're more likely to take action and stay motivated.

GET MOVING

Physical movement is one of the quickest ways to boost your motivation. When you move your body, it increases blood flow and releases endorphins, which help you feel more energized and positive. Even a few minutes of movement can make a big difference in how motivated you feel.

If you're feeling stuck or unmotivated, take a break to move around. You don't have to do a full workout—just a quick walk around the block, some stretches, or even dancing to your favorite song can help. The physical movement helps wake up your body and mind, giving you a fresh burst of energy to tackle the task at hand.

For example, if you're working at your desk and start to feel sluggish, stand up and do some stretches or take a quick walk. When you come back, you'll feel more refreshed and ready to focus. This simple hack works because it gets your body and brain out of the "stuck" mode and into action mode.

CONCLUSION

Quick Motivation Hacks for Fast Action

Motivation doesn't always come easily, but with the right hacks, you can find it quickly when you need it most. Whether it's using the 5-second rule to take immediate action, applying the 2-minute rule to make tasks feel smaller, or changing your environment to boost focus, these strategies help you get moving fast.

The key is to keep it simple. These hacks don't require a lot of time or effort, but they can have a big impact on your motivation. When you combine them with a positive mind-set, rewards, and small bursts of physical activity, you'll find that it's easier to overcome procrastination and get things done. The next time you're feeling stuck, try one of these quick motivation hacks and watch how fast you can jumpstart your energy and focus.

CONCLUSION:
LIVING A MOTIVATED LIFE

THROUGHOUT THIS BOOK, we've explored how to tap into your inner Motivation Force to get things done and achieve your goals. You've learned about the different drivers of motivation—pleasure, pain, importance, and certainty—and how to use them together to fuel your actions. We've also gone over quick hacks that you can use to get motivated when you're feeling stuck. Now, it's time to reflect on what you've learned and put it all together to live a motivated life.

Motivation isn't something you have to wait for. It's something you can create, control, and strengthen by using the tools in this book.

Motivation is like a fire, you can keep it burning by adding the right kind of fuel. When you stay connected to your purpose, use pleasure and rewards, build certainty, and make things easier and more fun, you'll always have the energy you need to take action.

Let's go over the key points from each chapter to remind you how to do this.

Chapter 1
THE MOTIVATION FORCE

In this chapter, we introduced the concept of the *Motivation Force*, which is the energy inside you that drives you to take action. We discussed how motivation is something you can tap into whenever you need it by understanding what makes you tick. By learning to harness this force, you can push yourself to get things done, even when you don't feel like it.

Chapter 2
WHAT IS MOTIVATION AND WHERE DOES IT COME FROM?

Motivation is when your desire to do something is so strong that it helps you overcome obstacles. This chapter explained that motivation comes from a combination of importance (how much you value something) and certainty (how confident you are that you can do it). When you increase the importance of a task and build your confidence in succeeding, motivation naturally follows.

Chapter 3
THE MAIN OBSTACLE TO MOTIVATION

This chapter focused on internal resistance, the tug of war inside of us between what we want to do and what we need to do. We talked about the *Motivation Seesaw*, where the stronger desire always wins. By learning to tip the seesaw in favor of the task, you can overcome procrastination and push yourself to take action.

Chapter 4

THE FIRST TWO GREAT MOTIVATION DRIVERS: PLEASURE AND PAIN

In this chapter, we explored the powerful motivation drivers of pleasure and pain. We naturally move toward things that feel good (pleasure) and avoid things that feel bad (pain). By associating tasks with the pleasure of achieving them and the pain of not doing them, you can create strong motivation to get things done.

Chapter 5

THE NEXT TWO GREAT MOTIVATION DRIVERS: IMPORTANCE AND CERTAINTY

Here, we dove deeper into importance and certainty. The more important something feels, and the more certain you are that you can succeed, the more motivated you'll be. By connecting tasks to your bigger goals and building your confidence, you can increase your desire to take action.

Chapter 6

THE POWER OF LINKING

This chapter introduced the concept of linking, which is the process of connecting tasks to things that already motivate you. When you link a task to something meaningful or enjoyable, it becomes easier to get started. We talked about how to use questions to create these links and make even boring tasks feel important and rewarding.

Chapter 7

MAKE IT MEANINGFUL: TAPPING INTO OUR IMPORTANCE DRIVERS

In this chapter, we discussed how to make tasks more meaningful by connecting them to your purpose, identity, and values. When a task reflects who you are and what you care about, it becomes easier to stay motivated. By tapping into your deeper importance drivers, you can make even routine tasks feel like they matter.

Chapter 8

MAKE IT CERTAIN: TAPPING INTO CERTAINTY DRIVERS

Certainty is a powerful driver of motivation. In this chapter, we talked about how building confidence in your ability to succeed can make tasks feel less overwhelming. We explored strategies for increasing certainty, like breaking tasks into smaller steps and looking at past successes.

Chapter 9

MAKE IT EASY: TAPPING INTO THE AVOIDANCE OF PAIN DRIVER

One of the main reasons we avoid tasks is that they feel hard or painful. This chapter focused on ways to make tasks easier, like breaking them into smaller parts, simplifying the process, and adding elements of fun. When tasks feel easy and manageable, we're less likely to avoid them.

Chapter 10

MAKE IT FUN, INTERESTING, EXCITING, AND SATISFYING: TAPPING INTO PLEASURE DRIVERS

Pleasure is a key driver of motivation. In this chapter, we looked at how to make tasks more enjoyable by adding fun and excitement. When a task is fun or interesting, it feels less like a chore and more like something you want to do. We also talked about how to find satisfaction and rewards in the process.

Chapter 11

IGNITE THE FIRE: COMBINING YOUR MOTIVATION DRIVERS

In this chapter, we learned how to combine all of the motivation drivers—pleasure, pain, importance, and certainty—to ignite a powerful fire of motivation. When you link tasks to things that matter, make them fun and easy, and focus on the rewards, you can create a strong push to take action. Combining these drivers helps you stay motivated over time.

Chapter 12

HACKS TO GET MOTIVATED QUICKLY

Sometimes, you need a quick boost of motivation. In this chapter, we went over some simple hacks like the 5-second rule, the 2-minute rule, and changing your environment. These hacks are designed to help you jumpstart your motivation when you're feeling stuck or unmotivated.

LIVING WITH MOTIVATION EVERY DAY

Now that you've learned all of these strategies, it's time to start living with motivation every day. The key to staying motivated isn't about waiting for the right mood to strike, it's about creating the right conditions for motivation. You can do this by using the tools in this book to keep your motivation fire burning strong.

Remember that motivation is a habit. The more you practice using these strategies, the easier it becomes to stay motivated in all areas of your life. Whether it's getting through daily tasks or working toward your biggest goals, you now have everything you need to keep moving forward.

STAY CONNECTED TO WHAT MATTERS

At the heart of motivation is purpose. When you stay connected to what matters most to you—your goals, values, and the people you care about—motivation comes naturally. Whether you're trying to achieve something big or simply handle your responsibilities, staying connected to your purpose will give you the energy to keep going.

Don't be afraid of challenges and setbacks. They're a normal part of the journey, and each one is an opportunity to grow and learn. By focusing on progress, staying flexible, and practicing self-compassion, you can overcome any obstacle and keep moving toward your goals.

EMBRACE THE JOURNEY

Motivation isn't about being perfect or always feeling energized. It's about embracing the journey, staying focused on what matters, and using the tools you've learned to create motivation when you need it. You now have the power to live a motivated life, full of energy, purpose, and achievement.

With these strategies, you can accomplish anything you set your mind to. Whether you're working on a big project, a personal goal, or simply managing your day-to-day life, you have the tools to keep your motivation fire burning bright. So go out there and live your most motivated life.

The Motivation Force is now yours to use.

ACTION PLAN: USING THE MOTIVATION FORCE

NOW THAT YOU'VE read this book, it's time to put what you've learned into action. To help you stay motivated and accomplish your goals, this action plan will guide you step-by-step. It will remind you of the key strategies from the book and show you how to use them in your daily life. Follow these steps to keep your motivation strong and get things done.

1. IDENTIFY YOUR PURPOSE

Before starting any task, think about why it's important. Ask yourself how this task connects to your bigger goals or values. When you know why a task matters, you're more likely to feel motivated to complete it.

- Write down your main goals and why they are important to you.
- For each task you face, ask yourself, "How does this help me reach my bigger life goals?"
- Keep your purpose in mind while working on each task to stay motivated.

2. USE THE 5-SECOND RULE TO START QUICKLY

When you need to start a task but feel stuck, use the 5-second rule. Count down from five—"5, 4, 3, 2, 1"—and then take action immediately. This stops your brain from overthinking and helps you move before hesitation sets in.

- Practice the 5-second rule whenever you feel like you're about to procrastinate.
- Don't wait for the perfect moment—just count down and start.
- The sooner you take action, the easier it will be to keep going.

3. BREAK TASKS INTO SMALL STEPS

Big tasks can feel overwhelming, so break them down into smaller, manageable steps. Focus on completing just one step at a time. This makes the task feel easier and helps you build momentum.

- List all the steps needed to complete your task.
- Focus on finishing just the first step, then move on to the next.
- Celebrate each small win to keep your motivation high.

4. MAKE TASKS FUN AND EASY

If a task feels boring or difficult, find ways to make it more enjoyable. Add fun elements, like listening to music or turning it into a game. You can also make tasks easier by simplifying them and removing distractions.

- Add something fun to your tasks, like playing music or setting a timer for short breaks.

- Remove distractions from your environment to stay focused.
- Find ways to enjoy the process, not just the result.

5. USE THE PLEASURE AND PAIN DRIVERS

To stay motivated, focus on both the rewards of completing a task and the pain of avoiding it. Think about how good you'll feel when the task is done and how relieved you'll be. Also, remind yourself of the negative consequences of not doing the task.

- Write down the benefits of completing your task and the consequences of not doing it.
- Keep these in mind as you work to stay focused and motivated.
- The stronger you feel about the pleasure and pain, the more motivated you'll be.

6. BUILD CERTAINTY AND CONFIDENCE

Certainty is key to staying motivated. Build your confidence by focusing on past successes and breaking tasks into smaller parts. The more certain you are that you can succeed, the easier it will be to start and finish tasks.

- Think about times when you successfully completed a similar task.
- Break the task into small steps and focus on completing each one.
- Each time you finish a step, remind yourself that you're capable of succeeding.

7. REWARD YOURSELF FOR PROGRESS

Rewards are a great way to stay motivated, especially for long or difficult tasks. Give yourself small rewards after completing each step or reaching a milestone. These rewards don't have to be big, but they should be something that makes you feel good.

- Set small rewards for yourself after each milestone.
- For example, take a short break, enjoy a treat, or do something fun once you finish a step.
- Use rewards to keep yourself motivated throughout the task.

8. CREATE A PLAN AND STICK TO IT

Having a clear plan helps you stay focused and organized. Write down all the tasks you need to do and create a schedule for completing them. Sticking to your plan makes the process easier and helps you measure your progress.

- List all the tasks you need to complete.
- Create a simple schedule that breaks these tasks into daily or weekly goals.
- Review your progress regularly and adjust the plan if needed.

9. HANDLE CHALLENGES WITH FLEXIBILITY

Challenges and setbacks are a normal part of life. When things don't go as planned, stay flexible and be willing to adjust. Instead of giving up, find a new way to approach the task or ask for help if needed.

- When you face a challenge, take a step back and find a new approach.
- Stay focused on your goal, even if you have to change your method.
- If you're stuck, talk to someone for advice or support.

10. KEEP MOTIVATION HIGH WITH SMALL WINS

Celebrating small wins is an easy way to keep your motivation going. Each time you complete a step or reach a goal, take a moment to acknowledge your success. These small victories help build momentum and make it easier to stay motivated.

- Set small goals for each task and celebrate when you reach them.
- Recognize your progress and remind yourself how far you've come.
- Use each small win to motivate you to keep moving forward.

CONCLUSION

Take Action and Stay Motivated

This action plan is designed to help you stay motivated, no matter what challenges you face. By using these simple strategies—like finding your purpose, starting quickly, breaking tasks down, making them fun, and rewarding yourself—you can keep your motivation strong every day. Remember, motivation is something you can create by using the right tools and habits.

Now, it's time to take action. Start by applying one or two of these steps to your current tasks, and see how they help boost your motivation. Keep practicing these techniques, and over time, living a motivated life will become easier and more natural. You have everything you need to succeed, so get started and enjoy the process!